Haiku
Ghazal
Sonnet
Lyric
Pastourelle
Pantoum
Cinquain
Sijo
Canzone
Ruba'i
Couplet

ARVON INTERNATIONAL POETRY COMPETITION 2010

Your entries are invited for
The Arvon Foundation's prestigious
open poetry competition

First Prize £7,500
Other Prizes Total £5,500

Judged by Carol Ann Duffy,
Elaine Feinstein & Sudeep Sen

Enter online at
www.arvonfoundation.org
by 16 August

P9-CEU-617

arvon   ARTS COUNCIL
             ENGLAND

The Arvon Foundation is a registered charity (Charity No. 306694)

GRANTA

12 Addison Avenue, London W11 4QR
email editorial@granta.com
To subscribe go to www.granta.com
Or call 845-267-3031 (toll-free 866-438-6150) in the United States, 020 8955 7011 in the United Kingdom

ISSUE III

EDITOR	John Freeman
DEPUTY EDITOR	Ellah Allfrey
ARTISTIC DIRECTOR	Michael Salu
ONLINE EDITOR	Ollie Brock
EDITORIAL ASSISTANTS	Emily Greenhouse, Patrick Ryan
ARCHIVE INTERN	Ted Hodgkinson
DESIGN INTERN	Daniela Silva
FINANCE	Geoffrey Gordon, Morgan Graver, Craig Nicholse
MARKETING AND SUBSCRIPTIONS	Anne Gowan, David Robinson
SALES DIRECTOR	Brigid Macleod
TO ADVERTISE IN THE UK CONTACT	Kate Rochester, katerochester@granta.com
TO ADVERTISE IN THE USA CONTACT	Emily Cook, ecook@granta.com
IT MANAGER	Mark Williams
PRODUCTION ASSOCIATE	Sarah Wasley
PROOFS	Katherine Fry, Lesley Levene, Jessica Rawlinson, Vimbai Shire
ASSOCIATE PUBLISHER	Eric Abraham
PUBLISHER	Sigrid Rausing

This selection copyright © 2010 Granta Publications

In the United States, *Granta* is published in association with Grove/Atlantic Inc., 841 Broadway, 4th Floor, New York, NY 10003, and distributed by PGW. All editorial queries should be addressed to the London office.

Granta USPS 000-508 is published four times per year (March, June, September and December) by *Granta*, 12 Addison Avenue, London W11 4QR, United Kingdom, at the annual subscription rate of £34.95 and $45.99.

Airfreight and mailing in the USA by Agent named Air Business, C/O Worldnet Shipping USA Inc., 149 – 35 177th Street, Jamaica, New York, NY 11434. Periodicals postage paid at Jamaica NY 11431. US POSTMASTER: Send address changes to Granta, PO Box 359, Congers, NY 10920-0359.

Granta is printed and bound in Italy by Legoprint. This magazine is printed on paper that fulfils the criteria for 'Paper for permanent document' according to ISO 9706 and the American Library Standard ANSI/NIZO Z39.48-1992 and has been certified by the Forest Stewardship Council (FSC). *Granta* is indexed in the American Humanities Index.

Granta is grateful to SLL/Sterling Lord Literistic, Inc. for permission to quote from 'The Truth the Dead Know', © Anne Sexton.

The Centre for Iris Murdoch Studies at Kingston University purchased the letters from Iris Murdoch to Raymond Queneau with donations from The V&A Purchase Grant Fund, The National Memorial Heritage Fund, The Friends of the National Libraries, The Breslauer Foundation (USA), Kingston University and The Iris Murdoch Society.

ISBN 978-1-905881-19-2

CONTENTS

7 **Missing Out**
Leila Aboulela

26 **Poem**
Nicholas Christopher

31 **The Book of the Dead**
Janine di Giovanni

56 **Poem**
Adrienne Rich

57 **Dyke Bridge**
Peter Orner

65 **Ceiling**
Chimamanda Ngozi Adichie

81 **The Last Thing We Need**
Claire Vaye Watkins

97 **One Hundred Fears of Solitude**
Hal Crowther

118 **Poem**
Seamus Heaney

119 **Letters**
Iris Murdoch

131 **Losed**
Joseph O'Neill

133 **Traces**
Ian Teh

169 **Property**
Elizabeth McCracken

189 **Lino**
Colin Grant

203 **High and Dry**
Richard Russo

231 **The Farm**
Mark Twain

246 Notes on contributors

MISSING OUT

Leila Aboulela

In his first term at college in London, Majdy wrote letters home announcing that he would not make it, threatening that he would give up and return. To call him on the phone, his mother made several trips to the Central Post Office in Khartoum, sat for hours on the low wooden bench, fanning her face with the edge of her *tobe* in the stifling heat, shooing away the barefooted children who passed by with loaded trays trying to sell her chewing gum, hairpins and matches. 'Get away from my face,' she snapped at the girl who had edged by her side and was almost leaning onto her lap. 'Didn't I just tell you I don't want your stuff?' On the third day she got through, wedged herself into a cubicle but did not close the glass door behind her. Majdy's throat tightened when he heard her voice. In the cool corridor of the hostel he held the receiver and leaned his head against the wall, hiding his face in the crook of his arm. The students who passed him walked a little bit quicker, felt a little bit awkward hearing his voice heavy with tears, unnaturally loud, foreign words they could not understand echoing and hanging around the walls.

There in Khartoum, she also, in her own way, could not understand what he was saying. All this talk about the work being difficult was, of course, nonsense. Her son was brilliant. Her son always came top of his class. She had a newspaper photograph of him at sixteen when he got one of the highest marks in the Secondary School Certificate, shaking the now-deposed president's hand. His father had slain a sheep in celebration and distributed the meat among the beggars that slept outside the nearby mosque. His sisters had thrown a party for him, heady with singing and dancing. And she had circled the pot of burning incense over his head, made him step over it, back and forth, to ward off the envy and malice that was surely cloaking him. Ninety-nine per cent in the maths paper, she had ecstatically repeated to friends and relations. Ninety-nine per cent, and mind you, they took that extra mark from him just from sheer miserliness, just so as not to give him the full marks.

'Take this thought of giving up out of your mind,' she said to him on the long-distance line.

'Can't you understand I've failed my qualifying exam?' The word 'failed' was heavy on his tongue. 'The exam I need to be able to register for a PhD.'

'So sit it again,' she insisted. 'You will pass *inshallah* and then come home for the summer. I myself will pay for the ticket. Don't worry.' She had independent means, that woman. And when she put the phone down, a project started brewing in her mind. She dawdled on her way home, plotting and wishing. A few hours later, refreshed from her siesta and the cup of tea with milk she always had at sunset, she gathered the family and launched a new campaign: 'My Poor Son All Alone In London Needs A Wife'. That was how Majdy came to marry Samra. After banging his head against books, working the proofs again and again, copying curvaceous lambdas, gammas and sigmas from the blackboard and into the whirling mass of his dreams, he was ready to sit for his qualifying exam. In June he flew to Khartoum. In July he received the good news that he had passed, and by the end of summer he was returning to London accompanied by his new bride.

All his life Majdy had known Samra, as a cousin of his sister's best friend, as the daughter of so-and-so. There was no sudden meeting between them, no adolescent romance. He had detached memories of her: a black-and-white photograph of a child squinting her eyes in the sun, standing with his sister and others in front of the giraffes' cage at the zoo. A teenager in a blue dress with her hair in a single braid, holding a tray of Pepsi bottles at a friend's engagement party. And the horrific story that had fascinated him in his childhood – Samra getting bitten by a stray dog and having to have thirty rabies injections in her stomach.

In 1985, he had seen her through grapevines, behind a carport over which the leaves climbed and weaved a criss-cross maze. He was pressing the doorbell of a house near the university, on one of the smaller side roads which housed the university's staff. On the main road, the students were demonstrating against the proposed execution of an opposition-party leader. While they were marching for justice, Majdy was searching for Professor Singh, lecturer in topology, to beg for a reference letter. It was for one of those numerous grants to do postgraduate research that he was always chasing. From where he was, he could hear the shouting. It came to him in waves, rising and falling, rhythmic and melodious. He could not make out the exact words.

They never let the students get very far; they never let them reach the marketplace where they would swell in numbers and cause a riot. Where other grievances and older pains would join the cry against the injustice of that one death. And deprivation might shake off its hypnotic slumber and lash out in the monotonous heat of the day. Down University Road until the first roundabout and then the tear gas would blind them, send them running back, tumbling through the dust and the fallen banners on the ground.

She was crying when she and her friend came running and stood underneath the carport of the house adjacent to the professor's. Crying from the gas and laughing. 'I tore my sandal, it's ruined,' he heard her say. She held it in her hand, the tears running in parentheses down her dust-coated face. Her *tobe* had fallen down, collapsed around her waist and knees, and her hair had escaped the one braid it was tied into and stuck out from her head in triangular spikes. At the nape of her neck, tight little ringlets glistened with sweat, dark and sleek. Laden with moisture, they lay undisturbed and appeared detached from everything else, the tear gas and the dust, her torn sandal, her fallen *tobe*. There was a *zeer* in front of the house and he watched her lift the wooden cover, fill the tin mug with water and begin to wash her face. She smoothed her hair with water, searched through it for hairpins which she prised open with her teeth and locked the wayward strands.

And all the time she was laughing, crying, sniffing. Chatting to her friend as they both pulled the ends of their *tobes* over their left shoulders, wrapped the material neatly in place and over their hair. 'This sandal is so ruined you can't even wear it as a slipper!' her friend said.

He felt cynical watching them, especially when, now that the demonstration was disbanded, other students passed by, cursing and spitting, with torn shirts and the pathetic remnants of their banners. He did not have the anger to demonstrate, he did not have the ability to enjoy the thrill of rebellion. And the next day, as he predicted, the futility of their action was exposed. Mahmoud Muhammad Taha was hanged on a Friday morning.

Later, or perhaps at the time he was looking at her through the vines, he thought, I could talk to her now. She would be approachable now, not formal or shy. She would yield to me now. And over the years we will talk of this day again and again and claim it was the start. But he let her go, rang the professor's bell and soon heard footsteps coming towards him from inside.

It is pointless to resist fate, impossible to escape its meanderings. But who knows how to distinguish fate's pattern from amid white noise? Years later when his mother led her campaign, the name Samra cropped up. His older sister was dispatched to test the waters. The reception was good. Prospective bridegrooms living abroad (it didn't matter where) were in great demand.

When they walked into his room in London, they quarrelled. But this was not because the room was small and designed for one student. He had applied for married students' accommodation but the university had yet to allocate them a flat. The tension started up as soon as she stepped out of the bathroom. There were droplets of water on her hair and her arms, the sleeves of her blouse rolled up. 'Where is your prayer mat?' she asked.

'I don't have one,' Majdy said. He was lying in bed enjoying his return to that particular quiet of London, the patch of moving grey sky he could see from the window, the swish of cars on wet roads. It was as if Khartoum had been grinding around him in a perpetual hum and now that humming sound was pleasantly absent.

'Well, what do you use instead?' She was already holding a towel. 'Where's the *qibla*?'

He would need to figure out the direction of the *Ka'ba*. From Britain, Mecca was south-east of course, because Saudi Arabia was south-east. So in this particular room, which direction should she face? Where exactly was the south-east?

'I can't believe it,' she said. 'You've been here a whole year without praying?'

Yes, he had.

'And Fridays? What about the Friday prayers?'

'I have classes that day.'

'Miss them.'

He sat up. 'Don't be stupid. Where do you think you are?' The quick hurt look on her face made him regret that he had called her stupid. He took her in his arms and said, 'It's not as if I'm finding the course so easy that I can play truant.'

She smiled and was keen to brush away her disappointment. He suggested an outing and they went by bus to the Central Mosque. There he bought her a red prayer mat and a compass which pointed to the direction of Mecca. She also picked up a booklet which listed the times of the prayers. Each month was on a page, the days in rows and the different prayers in columns.

Sitting next to him on the bus, she studied the booklet. 'The times change so much throughout the year!'

'Because of the seasons,' he explained. 'In the winter the day is very short and in the summer it is very long.'

'So in winter I will be rushing to pray one prayer after the other and in the summer there will be hours and hours between afternoon and sunset.' She said 'I' not 'we' and that seemed to him proper and respectful. She would forge ahead on her own whether he joined her or not. He was relieved that this outing to the mosque had satisfied her. Cheap and hassle-free. On a student budget, he could scarcely afford expensive restaurants or luxurious shopping trips. It was good that she was a simple Khartoum girl, neither demanding nor materialistic.

Still, she said that she wanted him to promise to change, to try harder and commit to the compulsory prayers. She was intent on influencing him but he was shy of the intimacy conversations about faith and practice evoked. After all, they did not know each other well and these were heady days of physical discovery, the smallness of the room making them bump and rub against each other. He was, naturally, the first man in her life and she was swayed between discomfort and pleasure, between lack of sleep and the feeling that all her girlhood and all her beauty had led to this. A honeymoon in London, her wedding henna still bright on her palms and feet. Majdy was, he had to admit to himself, captivated by the comforts and delights she offered, charmed by her looks and laughter. Then she would spoil it all by talking about religion, by reminding him that without these five daily contacts one was likely to drift off without protection or grace or guidance. Was he not a believer? Yes, in a half-hearted way he was, but he was also lazy and disinterested. Here in London, Majdy argued, praying was a distraction, an interruption and, most of all because of the changing times that followed the movement of the sun rather than the hands of the clock, praying was inconvenient. 'Don't talk to me about this again,' he finally said, drawing her towards him. 'Don't nag.'

In the days to come, when he became engrossed in his work again, he sensed her by his side, sympathetic, aware of his moods, sensitive to his needs, gentle and generous. Then she would move away to splash in the bathroom and come out to pray. She held the day up with pegs. Five prayers, five pegs. The movement of the sun was marked, the day was mapped and Majdy felt his life become more structured, his time more blessed. In their cramped room Samra's prayer mat took up a large portion of the floor, the old *tobe* she covered herself with dropped over it in a coiled heap. Sometimes, she reproached with a look or a word, sometimes she looked sad and worried on his behalf, but she continued to follow her own course, her own obligations, keen to preserve this practice even though she was away from home.

He wanted her to enjoy lively, civilized London. He wanted her to be grateful to him for rescuing her from the backwardness of Khartoum. He thought that, like him, she would find it difficult at first and then settle down. But the opposite happened. During the first months, she showed the enthusiastic approval of the tourist. Enjoyed looking at the shops, was thrilled at how easy all the housework was. She could buy meat already cut up for her. There were all these biscuits and sweets to choose from and they were not expensive at all. Even the pharmacies were stocked so full of medicine in so many different colours and flavours that she almost longed to be ill. Every object she touched was perfect, quality radiated from every little thing. The colour of hairpins did not chip under her nails like it had always done; chewing gum was not the brittle stick that often dissolved in her mouth at the first bite. Empty jam jars were a thing of beauty; she would wash them and dry them and not be able to throw them away. Biscuit tins, those she wanted to collect to take back home, her mother would use them to store flour or sugar. Or put her own baked cakes in them, send a tin proudly to the neighbour, and days later the neighbour would return the tin with her own gift inside.

She put on weight, she wrote happy letters home. Majdy showed her the university's library – so many floors that there were lifts inside and even toilets! They toured the shining computer rooms and she was impressed. She made him feel that he was brilliant, which deep down he knew he was all along. Then the days shortened, became monotonous. She was like the holidaymaker who was getting a little bit tired of her exotic surroundings. Everything around her began to feel temporary, detached from normal life. This happened when Majdy began to talk of getting a work permit once his student visa expired, of not going back after he got his PhD.

It was the continuity that she found most alien. It rained and people lifted up umbrellas and went their way; the shelves in the supermarket would empty and fill again. The postman delivered the mail every day.

'Don't your lectures ever get cancelled? Don't your lecturers get ill, don't their wives give birth? When the Queen dies, will they give everyone a holiday?'

'She'll die on a Sunday,' he would say, laughing at her questions. 'This is what civilization is, the security to build your life, to make something out of it. Not to be hindered all the time by coups and new laws, by sitting all day in a petrol queue. By not being able to get your ill child to a doctor because they are on strike.'

She listened carefully to everything he said. Would nod in agreement though her eyes remained wary. When she spoke of the future though, she would imagine they were going back, as if his hopes of staying in London were only dreams, or as if his hopes were an inevitability she wished to deny. 'I imagine you coming home early,' she would say, there would not be this endlessly long working day like here.

'We would sleep in the afternoon under the fan, its blades a grey blur, the sun so hard and bright that it would still be with us through the closed shutters. I would tease you about your students – are the girls pretty, do they come to your office after lectures and sweetly say, Ustaz, I can't understand this, I can't understand that? Ustaz, don't be so hard on us when you're marking our exams. And you would laugh at me and shake your head, say I'm talking rubbish but I would know from your eyes how much my possessiveness pleases you. The children playing on the roof would wake us up, their footsteps thudding over the hum of the fan. They are not allowed up there, it is not safe among the jagged green pieces of glass that ward off thieves. And you are furious with them; you go outside and throw your slipper at your son as he drops himself down from the tree, one foot balanced on the windowsill. He is the eldest, the instigator. But he is mischievous and ducks; you miss him and have to shout

BRING THE SLIPPER BACK. From inside I hear his laugh like cool tumbling water. You once bought a whip for this boy, you got it from the souk in Umdurman where they sell good whips, and you were quite pleased with yourself that day. You lashed it through the air to frighten the children with its snake-like power. But you did not have much of a chance to use it because he took it and threw it on top of the neighbour's roof and so it remained there among the fluffs of dust, razor blades and other things the wind carried to that roof. I would make tea with mint. By now the sun would have nearly set, it would be the hottest part of the day, no breeze, no movement, as if the whole world was holding its breath for the departure of the sun. Our neighbour comes over and you drink the tea together, he brings with him the latest gossip, another political fiasco; and you are amused, your good mood is restored. Your son behaves well in front of guests; he leaves his play, comes and shakes the man's hand. The sound of grief cuts the stillness of the evening, like a group of birds howling, circling and yapping with their throats. We guess it must be the elderly neighbour across the square; he has been in and out of hospital for some time. I grab my *tobe* and run, run in my slippers to mourn with them.'

'You are hallucinating, woman.' This was Majdy's answer. He had proof. 'Number one, I will never, with the salary the university pays its lecturers, be able to afford us a house or a flat of our own. Unless I steal or accept bribes and there is not much opportunity for either in my kind of work. We would probably live with my parents; my mother would get on your nerves sooner or later. You will complain about her day and night and you will be angry with me because you expect me to take your side and I don't. Number two, how will I ever get to the souk of Umdurman with no petrol. And there is unlikely to be any electricity for your fan. The last thing, why do you assume that nothing pleases me better than drinking tea and gossiping with the neighbour? This is exactly the kind of waste of time that I want to get away from. That whole atmosphere where so-called intellectuals spend their time arguing about politics. Every lecturer defined by his political beliefs, every promotion depending on one's political inclination and not the amount of research he's done or the papers he's published. My colleagues would be imagining that it is their responsibility to run the country. Debating every little thing from every abstract angle. The British gave it up, packed and left without putting up a fight, and somehow the Sudanese carry this air of pride, of belief that their large, crazy country will one day rise gracefully from its backwardness and yield something good!'

She sometimes argued back when he spoke like that. Accused him of disloyalty, a lack of feeling. Sometimes she would be silent for days, control herself and not mention either the future or the past. Then like one breaking a fast, she would speak, offer him memories and stories, and wait for him to take them. Wait with the same patience, the same serene insistence with which the little girls at the Central Post Office had offered pins and gum to his mother.

'I am not making this up,' she said one night as they walked on a side street sleek with rain and yellow lamplight. 'This really happened. After your mother phoned you at the Central Post Office she stood for an hour waiting for a bus or a taxi. None came; transport was bad that day because of the petrol shortage. The sun burned her head and she became exhausted from standing. So she walked to the middle of the road, stood right in the middle of the road, and raised her hand, palm upwards. She stopped the first car, opened the front door and got in. "My son," she said to the driver, "I am fed up of waiting for transport. And I can't move another step. For Allah's sake, drive me home, I'll show you the way." And he did drive her home even though it wasn't on his way. And as they chatted, he called her Aunt.'

And in July, the rain would make silver puddles. The sun disappearing for a day, the new smell of the earth. And there would be no work that day, no school. The cars stranded islands in the flooded streets.

'Because there are no proper gutters,' he would tell her. 'No drainage system and all those potholes. Remember the stink of the stagnant water days later. Remember the mosquitoes that would descend, spreading disease.'

'Silver puddles,' she would say, 'under a sky strange with blue clouds.'

Another memory. She offered it like a flower pressed into his hands. On the week before the wedding, they went to visit his uncle. The electricity cut and the air cooler's roar turned to a purr, its fan flapped and then all the sound died down. The sudden darkness, the sudden silence. They sat and listened to the gentle drip-drop sound of the water on the air cooler's fresh straw. Opened the windows to let in the faint night air and the scents from the jasmine bushes. Moonlight filled the room with blue-grey shadows. Outlines rose of the coloured sweets on the table, the ice melting in their glasses of lemon juice. While their hosts stumbled around in search of candles and lights, Majdy had leaned over and kissed her for the first time.

'But, Samra, do you want a power cut in London? Think of that – elevators, traffic lights, the trains. Chaos and fear. They would write about it in the newspapers, talk about it on TV. And in Khartoum it is an everyday event, another inconvenience, part of the misery of life. Defrosted fridges become cupboards with the food all soggy and rotting inside.'

Sometimes he looked at her and felt compassion. Felt that, yes, she did not belong here. Looked at the little curls at the nape of her neck, dry now and light, not moist with sweat, and thought that she was meant for brilliant sunsets and thin cotton dresses. Her small teeth made to strip the hard husk of sugar cane, her dimples for friends and neighbours. He could see her in idle conversation, weaving the strands of gossip with a friend. Passing the time in the shade of palm trees and bougainvilleas, in a place where the hours were long.

Most times though, he could not understand how she was not excited by the opportunities their new life held. How she could not admire the civilized way that people went about their business here, their efficiency and decency, ambulances and fire engines that never let anyone down. The way a cheque card could slide through a wedge

on the wall and crisp cash emerge. These things impressed her, but
not for long. She exclaimed at how the pigeons and ducks in the
parks were left unmolested. No one captured them to eat them. But
instead of enjoying their beauty, she brooded over how poor her own
people were.

He began to think of her homesickness as perverse. Her reluctance
wholeheartedly to embrace their new life, an intransigence. He
began to feel bored by her nostalgia, her inability to change or to
initiate a new life for herself. Homesickness was blocking her
progress, blinding her to all the benefits she could gain. There were
so many choices, so many new doors and yet she was stuck in the
past, adoring Sudan and missing out on the present. He had, in the
time he had spent in London, met Sudanese women who blossomed
in their new surroundings. He had seen them in tight trousers they
would not dare wear back home, playing with lighted cigarettes in
their hands. And though he did not expect or really want her to do
exactly these things, he was disappointed that she did not capture
that same spirit and instead seemed shyer, more reserved than
she ever was in Khartoum. She wanted to wear her *tobe,* to cover
her hair and he would say no, no, not here. I do not want us to be
associated with fanatics and backwardness.

It is frightening to come home at the end of the day and find
your wife sitting, just sitting, in her dressing gown and her hair
uncombed just as you have left her in the morning. She, who checks
her reflection in every mirror, who for you scents her hair with
sandalwood, dips steel in kohl to wipe the rims of her eyes. You find
her sitting and the whole place is untouched, no smells of cooking,
the bed unmade, mugs stained with tea, the remaining few flakes of
cereal swollen in their bowl. She is silent, looks at you as if you don't
exist, does not yield or soften under your touch. Stroke her hair and
rub her hands and probe for the right words, the words she wants to
hear. Talk of jasmine-scented gardens, of a wedding dance, of the
high Nile breaking its banks. Until she can cry.

For days afterwards, as Majdy put his key in the lock, as he turned it, he would brace himself for that same scene, he would fear a reoccurrence. He had been happy that day. While she sat at home with a frozen heart, he had glimpsed a modest success, a slight breakthrough in his work. A paper he had been looking for, a paper written five years ago in his same area of work, was located in another library. And he had gone there, to that college on the other side of London, an event in itself, for he was always at the library or using the mainframe computers. He had found it, photocopied it, warmed to its familiar notation and travelled back, full of appreciation for that meticulous body of knowledge, the technology that enabled one to locate written material. We are centuries behind, he would tell her later, in things like that we are too far behind ever to catch up. And while she had sat in her dressing gown, immobile, ignoring hunger and thirst, he had entered the mind of that other mathematician, followed his logic and when finding an error (the subscript for lambda should have been t-1 and not t), a typing error or a more serious slip from the writer, he had been infused with a sense of pleasure. So that even while he knelt next to her and asked, what is wrong, what has happened, the formulae with their phis and gammas and lambdas still frolicked in his brain and the idea occurred to him that her name, if he ignored its real Arabic meaning, sounded just like these Greek letters, these enigmatic variables with their soft shapes and gentle curves. Alpha, lambda, sigma, beta, *samra.*

He proposed a practical solution to her problem. She must do something with herself, she was too idle, and as she was not allowed to work without a permit, then she must study. Already her English was good so word processing would be ideal; she could type his thesis for him. He was enthusiastic about the idea; a word-processing course of a few weeks, and through it perhaps she would meet others like herself from all over the world, make friends and keep busy. So she, who had once braved tear gas, the crush of running feet, now faced a middle-aged teacher, a jolly woman who had recently travelled to Tunisia for her holidays and come back encased in kaftans and shawls. The teacher gushed at Samra, 'You must be so relieved that you are here, all that war and famine back home. You must be relieved that you are not there now.' From such a woman Samra recoiled and like a spoiled stubborn child refused to continue with the course.

Out of exasperation, Majdy suggested that she should go home for a few months. He winced as he saw her try to hide the eagerness from her voice when she said, 'Yes, that would be nice.' And the polite questions, wouldn't the ticket be too expensive, would he be all right on his own? Then she left, easily, so easily as if she had never truly arrived, never laid down roots that needed pulling out.

Without her, it suddenly started to feel like the year he had spent alone in London before they got married. The days drifting together, no reason to come home in the evening, all around him too much quietude. Without her he was not sure how to organize his day, to work at home or at the library, to work late at night or wake up early in the morning. He knew it did not matter either way but that early sparkle of liberty which had characterized the first days of her absence, that feeling of relief, of a responsibility shed, soon faded away and freedom hung around him, stale and heavy.

While Samra was away, London became more familiar to him. He thought of it as his new home and it was as if the city responded. He could feel it softening around him, becoming genial in its old age. The summers getting hotter and hotter. A new humid heat, sticky, unlike the dry burning of the desert in Sudan. People filled the streets, the parks, a population explosion or as if a season of imprisonment was over and they were now let loose. They lay immobile on towels spread on the grass, drove in cars without roofs, spilled out of cafes on to the pavements.

Beggars squatted around the stations, Third World style. The sight of the beggars jarred him, he could not look them in the face, he could not give them money. It did not look right or feel right that white people should be poor. It was shameful that they were homeless and begging. It was unnatural that he was better off than them. He had a faint memory of discovering that in Europe begging was illegal. The information, incredible to him and awe-inspiring, had been in his mind part of the magic of the Western world. A place where everyone's livelihood was so guaranteed that begging could be considered a crime.

He had once told Samra that this country chips away one's faith, but he began to see that it chipped away indiscriminately at all faith, even faith in itself. And as it accepted him, his admiration for it stabilized, his faith in it wavered. It was no longer enough, as it once had been, that he was here, that he was privileged to walk London's streets, smell the books of its libraries, feast his eyes on its new, shining cars. He would walk on wet roads that never flooded and realize that he would never know what it would be like to say, 'My ancestors built this, my grandfather borrowed a book from this library.' London held something that could never be his, that was impossible to aspire to.

His mother phoned him, her voice loud over the bustle of the Central Post Office. 'Why did you send Samra back for a holiday so soon? Is anything wrong between you?'

He was taken aback. 'No, of course not.' Marrying Samra had helped him feel settled and comfortable, well fed and looked after. He had liked working late into the night, kept company by her presence, the click of the spoon as she stirred sugar in tea, the chiming of her bangles, her movements when she stood up to pray in that early summer dawn. 'Did she complain about anything?'

'No.' His mother's voice was casual. 'She just mentioned that you don't pray.'

'Oh.' He could not think of a reply. The corridor of the hostel was empty. He stared at the vending machine which sold chocolates and drinks. Samra had been fascinated by this machine. She had tried to get it to work with Sudanese coins. He missed her.

'Is it true that you want to stay on in London after you get your degree?' This was why she had telephoned. The nip of anxiety.

'Yes, it would be better for me.' His PhD was now within reach. He had been invited to a conference in Bath, he was stepping through the door, and after all this hard work, he intended to stay and reap what he had sown.

His mother gasped down the line, 'How can you leave me all alone in my old age?'

He smiled because he had brothers and sisters living in Khartoum. There was no need for her melodramatic response. 'Don't you want the best for me? You are the one who is always complaining that Sudan is going from bad to worse.'

His mother sighed. First he had threatened to abandon his studies and return without a degree, now he was threatening the opposite! She had married him off so that he would not drift away, so that he would stay close. 'But what if things improve here, son? If they strike oil or make lasting peace, would you not be missing out?'

'I can't decide my future based on speculations.' Simulate a system over time, build a model, play around with a set of variables, observe what happens when you introduce a shock. This was his work.

Back in his room, Majdy noticed the silence. The floor looked strangely larger. Samra had folded her prayer mat and put it away in her side of the cupboard. She had not needed to take it with her. In Khartoum there were plenty of other mats. Mats with worn faded patches in those places where people pressed their foreheads and stood with wet feet. Majdy opened the cupboard and touched the smooth, velvet material. It stirred in him a childish sense of exclusion, of being left out, like a pleasure he had denied himself and now forgotten the reasons why. She had held the day up with pegs; not only her day but his too. Five pegs. And now morning billowed into afternoon, into night, unmarked. ∎

"**Brilliant . . . One of the most profound and devastating novels ever to come out of Vietnam—or any war.**"

—SEBASTIAN JUNGER, front page of
The New York Times Book Review

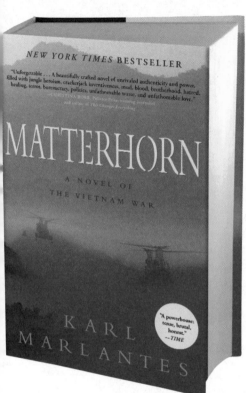

"Powerful . . .
Matterhorn **will take your heart, and sometimes even your breath, away.**"
—ALAN CHEUSE,
San Francisco Chronicle

"I've laughed at *Catch-22* and wept at *The Thin Red Line,* **but I've never encountered a war novel as stark, honest, and wrenching as** *Matterhorn.* **. . . I found it nearly impossible to stop reading.**"
—MICHAEL SCHAUB,
National Public Radio

"**Here is storytelling so moving and so intense that there were times I wasn't sure I could stand to turn the page. . . .** There has never been a more realistic portrait or eloquent tribute to the nobility of men under fire. Vladimir Nabokov once said that the greatest books are those you read not just with your heart or your mind but with your spine. This is one for the spine." —MARK BOWDEN, author of *Black Hawk Down*

Over 150,000 copies in print after seven printings
In Bookstores Now

ATLANTIC MONTHLY PRESS
AN IMPRINT OF GROVE/ATLANTIC, INC.
DISTRIBUTED BY PUBLISHERS GROUP WEST

In association with
EL LEÓN LITERARY ARTS
www.groveatlantic.com

On Jupiter Place

After my mother was diagnosed
with tuberculosis I lived
in one of the identical
brick houses on a long street
with my grandfather who worked
twelve-hour days six days a week
and my grandmother
who was too restless
to stay home for long
so that I was left on my own
at age four with plenty of time
to meet the neighbours
Mr Porti the building inspector
who died of a heart attack
behind the wheel of his Plymouth
and Mr Cleary the Con Ed linesman
with the Marine Corps tattoo
who chainsmoked Camels
and his beautiful daughter Nora
the nurse in her crisp uniform
who worked the night shift
and walked home from the bus stop
every morning at eight
and his son Neal Jr arrested
in Chinatown with a truckload

of stolen fireworks
and four doors down
Mrs Kornstein whose husband
was gassed at Auschwitz
where she received
a different sort of tattoo
the jagged numerals on her wrist
that she refused to remove
and two doors down from her
behind a wall of evergreens
Mr Boehringer the baker
a Bund member during the war
who spoke only German at home
and told anyone willing to listen
including his granddaughter
Heidi with her blonde pigtails
that Franklin Roosevelt was a Jew
in league with Stalin –
Heidi who ate uncooked
hot dogs without buns
they tasted like bologna she said
which was what the Lazzeri twins
Vincent and Little Steve
piled on Silvercup bread
with no mustard or mayo
their father Big Steve a mobster
who every Christmas
gave his wife a fur coat
and on their tenth anniversary
a two-tone Coupe de Ville
that he washed and waxed

on Sundays in their driveway
next door to Mr Porti's family
struggling behind drawn drapes
his daughter Genevieve
in hand-me-down dresses
and scuffed shoes was my friend
her mother the widow
had suffered a nervous breakdown
so that Genevieve too
was being raised by her grandmother
herself a widow born in Sicily
who carried a cane to ward off dogs
and across the street from them
Mr Fallon the used-car salesman
who had no licence
and was driven to work
by his wife a secret drinker
that everyone knew about
both of them tormented
by their roughneck son
who one day put me
in a headlock until I turned blue
and I knocked his tooth out
and bloodied his nose
and his mother screamed that I was a savage
that we were all savages
though in fact I rarely got into trouble
and mostly kept to myself
while my father all that time
lived alone in the small apartment
that had been our home

before my mother was hospitalized
and held down two jobs
one to support us
the other to pay her medical bills
until finally she was released
from the hospital
and that first afternoon was resting
in my grandmother's room
when I was brought in to her
I hadn't seen her in a long time
she was pale and very thin
her hair was cut short
and I told her to get out
of my grandmother's bed
out of her room
I didn't know who she was anymore
maybe I never did or could –
not the girl who danced
until dawn on her wedding night
or the middle-aged woman
with ailments real and imaginary
who withered beneath
the weight of her fears –
for when she died many years later
having loved me (I know) as best she could
she was still a stranger

GRANTA

THE BOOK OF
THE DEAD

Janine di Giovanni

I always begin bedtime stories to my son the same way: 'Once upon a time, a long, long time ago . . .'

And he always finishes, because, like me, he is impatient: 'In a place far, far away . . .'

Every time I fly into Sarajevo, and my plane cruises low over Mount Igman, crushing the thick, grey clouds, I hear that fairy-tale voice inside my head: Once upon a time, in a place not so far away, a city on the river, a city in Europe at the end of the twentieth century, fell under siege.

It was a time of great darkness for the people. Inside the city, which was surrounded by mountains, there was no water, electricity, heating, petrol, food or comforts. Packs of hungry wild dogs roamed the streets, picking up pieces of human flesh. Hundreds, sometimes thousands of artillery shells fell on the once-beautiful city on the river, which was smashed to pieces, and evil snipers perched on hillside mounts, taking aim at women and children running across the street. The soft flesh of knees and thighs was particularly vulnerable: easier to hit.

Surgeons operated by candlelight, or with miners' flashlights attached on their heads, and tried to keep their hands steady as the artillery rocked the foundation of the hospitals. People burned their books to keep warm and gathered twigs in the city parks. The elderly died in their beds, freezing to death, alone, clutching at dirty sheets. An old man was shot between the eyes by a particularly accurate sniper. He had been chopping wood to heat an old people's home that was on a front line that everyone – including the United Nations who were there to keep the peace – had forgotten about.

As for the children who came of age during this siege, they learned to live with fear, to comfort their parents during artillery attacks, and to understand madness. Schools stopped and time froze. There were no birthday parties, no cakes made with fresh eggs, no chocolate bars, no Christmas trees for the Christians or toys for the Muslims at Bajram, or play dates or singalongs. There was no future and there were no dreams.

And no one came to save these people, not for a long, long time.

Once upon a time, in the city on the river, 11,000 people were killed, 1,598 of them children. Some 19,000 people were injured and the damages were nearly always horrific: gunshot wounds, amputations and paralysis.

There were so many stories. The young teenage swimmer who lost her breast. The boys who loved soccer who lost feet, legs. The girl who became Miss Sarajevo dyeing her hair with lye. And there was an eight-month-old baby, Kemal. During the shelling, his mother threw her body over his in an attempt to protect her infant. She died instantly, and Kemal had such a grave wound that his right leg had to be amputated at the knee. Kemal's grandmother found the tangle of blood and bones and flesh in a field and the baby was eventually evacuated to Italy, separated from his family for five years.

There was nowhere that was safe, because living in Sarajevo was like being in a doll's house with a giant perched above it, holding great boulders that he would drop on the house, squashing the people, just for fun. Some people decided to defy it, to stay inside for the entire siege, not to leave their reinforced apartments. But even they were not safe: one day, a stray bullet would fly through the window as they were trying to wash dishes with a few cups of water that they had stood in line for hours to get. And then they were dead.

Of course, life also continued during these thousand days, because it had to. While people went slowly mad during the siege, people also fell in love, made love, and made babies.

'I felt healthy as an ox during the siege, my sex life was fantastic,' a good friend told me later. 'I never got sick during the siege. My adrenalin was pumping too high, my immune system was perfect.'

Children were born and baptized. I held my baby godson in my arms at the Catholic cathedral one December morning and he screamed and screamed as water was poured on his head, and afterwards we celebrated with rice, bread, cake and chocolate bars bought on the black market. People married, people wrote poetry, people drank and smoked a lot, and a very few lucky ones died of natural causes. Those who stayed put throughout the siege were bound together by a terrible solidarity: they had survived.

And so I returned, many years after the war was finally ended by a schizophrenic peace accord – fifteen years later to be exact. But the city on the river is not the same. There are new people who made money overseas and arrived after the war, picking at the bones of the city's skeleton, building ugly blue-glassed high-rise buildings and shopping centres.

There are refugees from eastern Bosnia who can never return home because their villages were burned down and the new inhabitants are the men and women who did it, who raped their wives and daughters and killed their husbands. There are foreign diplomats and their wives. There are people running glitzy hotels, boutiques, casinos, and more mosques than I thought possible, built by foreign money.

And of course, there are the spirits of the dead, which hang for me like the low grey clouds that always float around Balkan cities, particularly in the winter. I see the dead everywhere I go: not just in the enormous cemeteries created out of football fields during the war, but in the cafes where I once sat, in the Holiday Inn where the windows were all smashed by explosions, in front of the parliament building, the library, the old beer factory. I see them everywhere.

Those lucky enough to exit the siege of Sarajevo alive fell into several categories. There were those who left physically intact, and could rejoice, on some level, that at least they were alive even if they had endured days of hell. There were the injured and maimed, who still navigate the streets on shaky prostheses or in wheelchairs.

There are those who lost several, or all, members of their family. And there are those who may not show the scar of the shrapnel still lodged in the brain, or the thigh, or the shattered tibia or the jawbone shot off by a sniper, but those whose scars and wounds are deeper.

A psychiatrist in Kosevo Hospital, which stayed open during the siege and operated valiantly without electricity, even when the generators went off, once told me that at the height of the war the city was a walking insane asylum.

Another told me that 90 per cent of the war survivors in the city today had post-traumatic stress disorder.

Another told me to do myself a favour and move forward, forget the past. Say *dovidenja, Bosna*. Goodbye, Bosnia.

But I want to remember. I cannot help but remember. And so, coming back, flying from Ljubljana in the slick Slovenian jet cruising over Mount Igman – at one time the only exit route out of the siege – I looked down and tried to see the tunnel which had served as the sole route for supplies coming in and out of the city. I scanned the ground near the suburb Butmir, across from the landing strip of the airport, but could not see it.

I began to think of all I had lost, and all I had left behind, and I decided I must try to find – if he wanted to be found – Nusrat.

By the winter of 1993, I was beginning to go a little crazy, along with the 300,000 inhabitants of Sarajevo. The war that everyone thought would be over in a few weeks was dragging on in the brutal Balkan winter. The American flags that some families had hung from their frozen windows when a rumour went around the city that the Americans were coming to save them were beginning to look a little tattered and sad. Perhaps even a little mocking. Everyone was beginning to think the world had forgotten them.

My friend Mario, a poet, who had been caught in several artillery attacks, but survived, saw a woman's shoe full of blood in the snow one day. He rarely talked, but that day, he told me sombrely,

'You can kill a life without killing anyone . . . You can take a city, but you don't snipe people, you don't butcher people, you don't burn down villages.' He began to sob and I sat next to him in his freezing house knowing he was slowly going insane, but powerless to do anything except offer him another cigarette.

My friend Gordana saw a dog running with a human hand in its mouth. My friend Aida said, 'We are all falling down Alice in Wonderland's rabbit hole.' She remembers that first day of war in May 1992: she was walking down the street in her high heels and ponytail on her way to work when a tank came up behind her. As she crouched behind a trash can to take cover, she realized she was entering a new place from which she would probably never return. A few weeks later, Aida was forced to send her mother and her two-year-old son, Igor, on the last bus leaving Sarajevo for Germany, and they were separated for four years.

'Down that rabbit hole of the siege was a black-and-white world, and nothing inbetween,' she remembers. 'Like Alice's world. There was a Red Queen and a White Queen. And that is how the madness began . . .'

My home on the fourth floor of the Holiday Inn on Sniper's Alley had plastic windows that came from UNHCR aid packets. On one side of the ugly, Communist-era room was my flak jacket and my helmet with my blood group taped to it. On my shrapnel-chipped desk was a battery-operated Tandy, a high-street precursor to a laptop, a flashlight, a box of candles, four lighters, a box of chocolates and three bottles of water.

Physically, I was deteriorating. I had grown accustomed to not washing and I wore the same clothes several days in a row. Oddly enough, even though no one washed in those days, no one seemed to smell. Once a week, I bribed the men who guarded the hotel kitchen with a few packs of Marlboro Lights for a pot of hot water, and with that, I would set aside an hour to wash my hair. One night, in a fit of despair, I had chopped off my long thick hair with a pair of borrowed manicure scissors and although I looked odd, it made my life easier.

My view out of the plastic window was of a wasted, gutted city of burnt-out buildings and metal canisters that were used to deter the snipers. It was so cold that my skin peeled off when I took off my layers of clothes. I was living on a diet of chocolate bars I had brought in from Kiseljak – the Las Vegas frontier town that was the last stop before besieged Sarajevo – whisky, vitamins and cigarettes.

To this day, I cannot forget that cold. My internal barometer changed forever. The large, cavernous, Soviet-style unheated rooms where we would interview doctors or politicians; the freezing cold houses where people sat huddled and frightened around an oil stove; the ugly interior of the lobby of the Holiday Inn, where one afternoon I came back to see journalists abseiling down from the roof with ropes. Ice-crusted, breathing out slow breaths of frozen air.

I shivered when I woke in my sleeping bag, I shivered when I climbed out and slipped into the same clothes on the floor, and I shivered climbing back into the bag at night, to read by candlelight. Bizarrely, uniformed maids came every day to make up the beds – that is, to pat down the sleeping bags and to move around the dust. There was not much they could do without water. The toilets did not flush and nothing came out of the taps.

I was mentally fried. Every day people came to me with some kind of request: get me out of here, take a package to my sister, take my child to Germany, give me some money for firewood. There was only so much I could physically do in one day, and when I did not, Catholic guilt preyed on me ferociously.

The worst was the knowledge that I could leave whenever I wanted to, and they could not. My friend Corinne kept reminding me I was not a social worker but a journalist. But for all of us living in that place, that time, it was impossible not to blur the lines.

To compensate, I had little routines that kept me sane, like someone stricken with obsessive-compulsive disorder. One was to visit the morgue, every day. I usually did this in the morning, when Alija Hodzic, a pleasant Muslim man in his early fifties who ran the morgue, was still in a talkative mood. By the time I arrived, Alija would have counted the dead who came in overnight from the front lines and the hospitals, closed their eyes, tried to straighten their limbs, or if there were no limbs, tried to piece together the ravages of an artillery or sniper attack.

'Everyone else was afraid of the dead,' he would tell me later. 'But I never was. The dead cannot hurt you.'

After he arranged the bodies on slabs, and closed their eyes, he would then take out an ordinary notebook and carefully write down the names of the dead. This was important. Alija is a simple man, born in eastern Bosnia, a farmer at heart, but he believed in his job and he believed that the dead deserved some respect, especially during wartime. So he wrote their names, and where the bodies had arrived from, in simple school notebooks. By the end of the war, there was a stack of twenty-four notebooks, some brown, some green, some bound with yellowing Scotch tape.

If the dead had been killed in an attack in the city, he wrote '*grad*'. If they had died after being treated in the hospital, he wrote the unit they came from – 'C3' meant surgery. Soldiers were given the names of the front lines where they were killed – Stup, Otes, Zuc – and you could always tell where the fighting was heaviest overnight by how many were killed. There were a few 'NN's written down – *Nema Imena* – person unknown.

Alija did not fear the corpses, he prepared them for their funerals. But his assistant, Ramiz, was afraid. The poor man drank himself into a stupor before, during and after his work simply in order to be able to do his job. Even then, he did not do his job very well.

'It was no use having Ramiz around,' Alija said. 'I might as well have worked alone.' Once, when there was electricity at the Kosevo Hospital – a rare occurrence – the two men had to go to the top floor to collect some bodies. The power went out, and they were stuck for hours in the small space. Ramiz stank of booze from a binge the night before, or possibly even that morning.

'I kept asking him why he did it, why he was drinking himself to death,' Alija says. 'I did the same work and I did not have to drink to do it.'

But Ramiz looked at him woefully.

'What can I do?' he said. 'It's a war.'

This was a common expression in Sarajevo during the siege. Every possible question, from 'Why don't you love me anymore?' to 'Why are you cheating on your wife?' was answered with the same response. 'What we can do? It's a war.' It was a refrain repeated over and over by priests, doctors, soldiers, commanders, politicians, aid workers, mothers, teachers: they all said the same thing. What we can do? It's a war.

I remember Ramiz well. He was bad-tempered and day by day appeared to grow more nutty inside the morgue, and was certainly always drunk. But he survived. The snipers who aimed at people running across Marsala Tito Street did not hit him. He dodged all the shells that struck the city centre.

But he killed himself a few years after the war, hanged himself with a rope. Alija is not really sure why, but he reckons the alcohol, the memory of those dead bodies and probably a bad love affair finally got to Ramiz.

Some days at the morgue were worse than others. During the first months of the war, Alija remembers fifty or sixty people being brought in a day. There were the terrible days of massacres – the bread-line massacre, the water-line massacre, the market massacres – these were days when people went out to get food or supplies and were targeted, deliberately, by Serbs.

There were days when children were brought in, groups of them. Alija hated those days. That was when the children went outside to play, as happened one snowy morning in 1993, because they could not bear to sit in their apartments anymore. You can see the scene: the tired, frightened mother and her children begging her to go outside for some fresh air. So they go, because, really, no one but a monster would send an artillery shell into a group of kids building a snowman.

But they did. Alija was there the day the children came in from Alipasino Polje, the kids who were playing in the snow, and died from it. That was a bad day.

But the worst day of all was the day he came in and found his son, his beloved son, his oldest son, the boy who could do anything, lying dead on the slab. Ibrahim. Twenty-three years old, about to become a father in three months. Alija was late to work that day. He remembered he took his breakfast, some bread that tasted like sawdust, and some tea, and wandered down the hill from his house, avoiding the usual places where snipers could see him.

When he climbed the hill towards Kosevo Hospital, and made his way to the morgue, he saw a crowd outside. What's this? he thought, getting impatient. What do they want? Then he saw people he knew, some of his son's friends. It's Ibrahim, he thought quietly, and went into the morgue. Everything went black.

'I just passed out,' he says.

Eighteen years later, I find Alija and he recognizes me instantly. He is retired and now lives on a hill above Sarajevo in a house he once built for his son and spends his days tending to his cows. He is now sixty-four and could have worked a few extra years, but he feels that he has seen enough.

We leave the cows and sheep and go to his house and his wife, whose face is still etched with pain, makes us fresh juniper juice and heavily sugared Bosnian coffee. Their home is full of wood and light and is spotlessly clean. We sit, and we talk, and he remembers everything. The death of his son, that day, that time.

His daughter-in-law gave birth to a little boy a few months after Ibrahim was buried. The little boy is now seventeen. He looks just like his father did, and acts like him, and Alija can sometimes squint his eyes a bit and pretend it is his lost son.

My wartime routine rarely varied. Around midday, I made my way up the hill of Bjelave to the Ljubica Ivezic orphanage. This was a strange and terrible place. When the war started, everyone had run away except the donkey-faced director, Amir Zelic. I did not like him, nor him me, but for some reason, he would let me in and allow me to poke around. There were some days he kicked me out, but most of the time he seemed not to care. He asked me for cigarettes and disappeared.

Sometimes Amir was there, sometimes he was not, but no matter what, the children ran completely wild. Not only were they abandoned or orphaned, but many of them were mentally disturbed by trauma, neglect or learning disabilities. When the shelling started, especially when it happened at night – particularly terrifying, because there was no electricity so they lay in the dark with the whistle of the shells getting closer – they howled like dogs.

There were some older, truly crazed kids there, and one wintry day, they locked me in a room for a few hours and I had to climb out over a transom. If you approached them, they wanted cigarettes, money, drugs and food. They shouted, 'Fuck you, bitch! Welcome to hell! Whore! Fuck you!'

The little ones seemed to get completely lost in the shuffle. They were dirty, smelly and pitiful. If you tried to hold them, they flinched. I never knew, but I am sure, that there was terrible abuse going on when no one was looking – which was more or less all the time.

To eat, there was rice and strawberry yogurt powder twice a day, which Amir would proudly show me. There were rats, and rain poured through the broken windows. The floors were oily and damp and it smelled. The children slept eight or nine to a room, on piles of rags or clothes. There were no toilets, and they scratched with dirt and lice and neglect.

One day I found Nusrat Krasnic. He was nine, and looked more like a wild animal than a little boy. He was a Roma child (5 per cent of the Bosnian population are Roma) and had dark, matted skin and rather beautiful eyes. He was skinny as a rail, and dressed in thin cotton clothes in the middle of winter. Someone who had left or died passed on his boots, and they were too big.

What I remember the most – and what hurt me the most –

was that he wore socks on his hands in the middle of the biting, savage winter.

His mother and father had died during the war, in their house on Sirokaca Street. He had two brothers, and somehow they ended up at the orphanage at the beginning of the war – Amir was not sure.

'I can't keep track of these kids, it's a war!' he said gruffly when I tried to get information on Nusrat's family. Someone said his father might still be alive, and I went back to Sirokaca Street and asked around. No one had seen him. The neighbours told me. 'He's a Gypsy, they move around. Even during war.'

This is what I know, the only real facts because the police documented little during the war: Nusrat's mother, Ljubica, was killed when a shell crashed through the wall of their kitchen and reduced the entire house to a pile of rubble.

Nusrat knew the house was trashed, but at least once a week, he tried to get back. He ran away from the orphanage, and made the dangerous trek, crossing front lines and going too close to snipers' view, to get back home. Once he got pinned down for more than an hour inside a flowerpot on a bridge as a firefight raged around him.

Nusrat knew things, which he shared with me on long cold wintry days when we walked through the city together. He knew about *grenatas* – grenades – and what size they were. He knew how to jump on trucks and steal humanitarian aid packages to get extra food, and where to sell it. He knew what sniffing glue was, because the big kids in the orphanage did it. At night, he slept wrapped around his dog, Juju.

I forgot sometimes that he was a kid, because he was more like an old man. But he was only nine years old, and he still had it in him to want to play. So he and his brother Mohammed went sledding in the snow by holding on to UN trucks that passed and sliding along behind them.

Once in a while, he took me to the basement of the Hotel Europa, which had been bombed to pieces during the summer of

1992. Before the war, during the Hapsburg Empire, it had been the fashionable hotel for the well-heeled doing a Balkan tour. Once, inside the so-called Golden Visitor's Book, I found a page inscribed in 1907 in an elegant hand by an ancestor of a Bostonian friend. *Mrs HHH Hunnewell. Wellesley, USA.* I stared at it a long time. Was there ever a time when Sarajevo was a normal place?

Now, more than eighty years later, the Hotel Europa had lost its elegance – it was like being in Dante's ninth circle. Luckier refugees found bombed-out rooms and moved their meagre possessions inside, guarding their space jealously. The less fortunate hovered in the basement, which was full of water. Nusrat had some friends down there. An older refugee woman had taken in Nusrat and Mohammed, and tried to guide them, to protect them. But she could not control them: they ran away from her, she could not keep track of their movements, and eventually, she gave up.

The war had turned Nusrat savage. I tried to feed him, give him clothes and shoes, and give him tenderness, but I was aware always that I was temporary. He knew this too, with his animal-like sense, and so he did not get attached to me. I would go one day, and he would be back on the streets. I tried to teach him. Once I sat down with him and a book, but Nusrat had not been to school in a long, long time: before the war. He had forgotten how to write his name.

I left for a month to rest. I went to London and went to cocktail parties where people asked the same question: what is it like to get shot at? I could not enjoy myself, even with the marvel of hot water that ran through pipes. I stood under showers for an hour, till my skin rubbed raw. I ate real food, vegetables and fruit, and went into shops and remembered what it was like to have newspapers and telephones that had dial tones when you picked them up.

But then, I thought of Nusrat, and my friends inside the siege, and I felt guilty. I bought him clothes, and vitamins, and food. But when I returned in late April, when the water in the river was rushing high, and the spring military offensive was underway, and the Serbs were really kicking the shit out of Sarajevo, Nusrat had disappeared.

In the early months of 2010, about the same time of year that Nusrat and I used to run the gamut of the city front lines, I came back to Sarajevo, and I took a room in the Hotel Europa. It's now called Hotel Europe. Unbelievably, the old refugee centre has four stars and a high-end spa. My room overlooked a pub where slick young Bosnians partied all night without fear of getting shredded by artillery.

I took an elevator to the basement. The place where Nusrat and I huddled in the cold is now a gym with an elliptical machine and a sauna. There is a pool. The breakfast table groans with sausages, eggs, bread, different kinds of cheeses, imported meats. German businessmen crowded the table, stuffing their plates with rolls and honey. It almost hurt to look at the waste, remembering how the people I loved during wartime had hoarded a box of powdered milk, a tin of beef. And I began my hunt for Nusrat.

But no one seemed to know. The donkey-faced director, Amir Zelic, was still there, and he sent me a message through Velma, my interpreter: no Nusrat. Apparently, he had stayed on at the orphanage until four years ago – which would have made him twenty-three when he left – but no one had seen him since. The police had no record of his coming, or going.

But I was sceptical of Zelic, because he was involved in a scandal at the orphanage a few years back. There was a terrible fire and eight babies perished. No one seems to know the details, but Zelic was under investigation and therefore wary of talking to people like me. There were no records, he said firmly. That door was closed.

After the war, nuns from Zagreb came to Sarajevo and restored the Dickensian building to a beautiful white convent with hard, glistening wood throughout. It smelled of lemon oil. The nuns were neat and clean and took care of children in need. One Sunday morning, I sat with one of the sisters and she told me that they have tried to scour most of the memories of the war away, the way you wash a dirty floor. She showed me the neat chapel, the fresh flowers.

But on the other side of the convent, where they had moved the 'wild' kids, Amir was still in charge. This too had been renovated. People had heard about the orphanage during the war, and with donor money they rebuilt it and the rooms where the children sleep are now clean and light and full of toys. There is a room of babies, smiling, beautiful fat babies in cribs, with hanging mobiles of stars.

The morning I go to meet Amir, by chance, two men who guard the door tell me they know Nusrat well.

'He was here last week,' they said. 'He comes sometimes for breakfast.'

The last time they saw him, however, Nusrat was in terrible shape. He was homeless, and had taken to begging in the new parking lot in front of the Sanpaolo Bank. He spent the night outside, and the men told me they thought he was taking drugs. His brother, Mohammed, who had taken care of him in the orphanage (more or less) had died a few months earlier, from an overdose.

'He seems very ashamed of his life now,' one of the men told me. 'We tell him to come, have a shower, have a meal, but he only shows up once in a while.'

'When he is really desperate,' says the other man. They took my cellphone number to call me if Nusrat came back, and they told me where to go to look for him.

I thought of the little boy with dark eyes and socks on his hands. Could I have done more if I was not so burned out by that point? I was stricken with sadness. Then Amir came down and said, as though it had been a week and not fifteen years: 'You again. It's been a while.'

'Yes, a long time,' I said.

'Fifteen years,' he said, rubbing his girth. He had put on weight but otherwise looked the same. He called for hibiscus tea, coffee. A plate of biscuits appeared. He said he had gotten divorced. 'Who knows why? The war did terrible things to all of us.'

And Nusrat? I asked.

Amir nodded. Nusrat came in from time to time, he said, but he never stayed the night. He had been at the home until he was in his early twenties. The death of his brother had been a blow.

Was he taking drugs?

Amir shrugged. 'Most likely. I tried to get him jobs a while back, and he failed all the drug tests.'

I remembered the kid who showed me how to hook a hand over the back of the UN trucks and slide. I had lost him, in the same way I had lost my own brother, who died three years ago, because he had fallen through the cracks. You try to save people but sometimes it's like the *Titanic*: some people get on the life rafts and others do not. The ones who do get on always feel that they should have done more to pull the drowning aboard. I did not pull Nusrat aboard, and I did not pull my brother. I saved myself.

'What can you do?' he said, and I froze, thinking he was going to say, 'It's a war.' Instead he said, 'We could not save all of them.'

He was looking at his watch, but I asked for the records of Nusrat. He said there are none, 'and anyway, if there were, they belong to the state – confidential'. He asked me if I wanted a tour. We went up to see the babies, but Amir was in a rush. He would not let me hold any of them, even though they were all so very beautiful.

One day, back in wartime, Nusrat showed me a secret room in the orphanage, a room that was magically heated with oil heaters, and where there were several women in clean white clothes. Inside this room, there were also tiny, tiny babies.

We snuck inside, Nusrat and me, when the ladies were not there, and I held the babies. I sat in a hard wooden chair and, inexperienced with infants, shifted the infants from one shoulder to the next. Nusrat sat on the floor grinning. And that became another of our rituals: waiting until the ladies went to do something else, sneaking inside and holding the babies. They were warm and smelled clean. I began to feel something I had never felt before.

But one day we got caught, and the big woman in a white dress with those ugly white plastic Eastern European clogs they wear in Bosnia kicked us out. She locked the door, and told me if she caught me again near that room, she would tell Amir to ban me from the premises.

Later that day, Nusrat told me a secret. Those were the babies of the Muslim women who were 'touched'. He meant raped. The women who had been held in rape camps in Foca and other places east of Sarajevo, and raped and raped and raped, until they fell pregnant. An attempt, someone once told me, to wipe out their gene pool.

I found one of those rape babies when she was eight. Marina. She was delicate and ethereal, like an angel. I kept staring at her perfect, tiny, lovely face, unable to imagine that such a child could come from an act so violent. She went to school and had no idea her father was one of perhaps a dozen men who held her mother in a sports hall in Foca and raped her, one after the other.

While Marina was playful and sweet and was told that her father was a war hero killed during a battle, her mother was not so joyful. She was a train wreck of a human being, a shell of a body in a faded tracksuit. Her soul seemed to have been squeezed from her.

She shook and cried, she was full of shame and rage, she took tranquillizers to sleep and pills to fuel her up during the day. She rarely ate. And yet she still tried to protect her daughter, a child she had once wanted to abort because of the bad seed that had made her. But at the last minute, she realized the baby was half hers.

One early-spring day after I see Amir, I go to see Jasna. Jasna was in that hall with Marina's mother those awful days in the summer of 1992 in Foca, but she did not have a baby. She did not have a baby because when she was raped, over and over, nine times by her count, she was only twelve years old and did not yet have her period. Her mother was raped alongside her on one of these occasions. Neither mother nor daughter could help the other. The little girl screamed at the pain of losing her virginity to a soldier three times her age, and her mother was powerless to stop him. So she just lay there next to her little girl while the man pounded at her and the girl shrieked in agony.

Afterwards, when they brought them back, bloody, to the sports hall, they did not look at each other, and they never talked about it.

Today Jasna is thirty. She is a widow: her husband died three years ago, electrocuted on a job. She cannot bear children; she tried for several years and the doctors told her to give up. Her insides are scarred. She lives alone in a small room outside of Sarajevo that the state provides, but it's not permanent: any day, she says, she could be removed and then she is not sure where she will go.

She is without a man at the moment, and frankly, she tells me, it's fine. She says she does not like to think often of the days in 1992 when she was used like a punching bag by the Serb soldiers, or the day her father was taken away.

'They said: you will see him tomorrow,' she says. 'But we never saw him again.'

She pulls out photo albums, and I see a little girl, Jasna, before all this happened. She looks normal, like me at that age. The light has not yet gone out of her eyes. She wears shorts and smiles in a countryside shot. She sits with her younger siblings. She is walking to school. Then the photos stop.

She talks and tries to remember, but it's a merciful blur. Instead, she smokes, she smokes and she cleans her house. 'It stops you from thinking,' she says.

Velma and her boyfriend drive to the parking lot near the Sanpaolo Bank in Sarajevo late every night to look for Nusrat. But they don't find him. They ask people. I ask people. I go to places he might be. I try to find the old flowerpot where he hid during a shoot-out. When I leave, Velma – who is now in her twenties and grew up in central Bosnia during the war – promises she will keep looking.

I can't forget Sarajevo, I think, for Nusrat. If I forget Sarajevo, then it seems so much has been in vain. Instead, I go to see the man who knows best about memory, about the endless cycle of keeping track of remembering: Alija, and his book of the dead.

We meet again on a Friday morning, the Muslim day of prayer

and first day of the weekend. He's waiting for me in the early-morning light, in the parking lot of a cemetery past the tunnel where one of the few Bosnian tanks used to hide, draped in camouflage. He's squinting in the sunlight, wearing city clothes rather than his farming clothes: a neat pair of corduroys, a brown sweater, an ironed checked shirt. He takes me inside the office of the cemetery and a friendly secretary opens a drawer and takes out the books.

There are twenty-four books of the dead, and we begin at the beginning: July 1992, Alija's first day at work, when he took over the job at the morgue.

His hands, big and calloused, now used to dealing with the hides of his cows rather than the cold skin of the dead, stroke the covers of the books. He sits down, with great and heavy exhaustion, and sighs. He opens the first book, which already, only fifteen years after the war, seems very old.

The books are neat and orderly. He goes through them one by one, telling me about the things he remembers.

'This was my neighbour . . .' At another line, he points and drops his head. 'This was a young girl.' This was a soldier, this was an old lady, this was from that terrible massacre in the centre of town . . .

Finally, he gets to a page in October 1992. He takes out his handkerchief. He wipes his eyes. He runs his big hands over the page. His eyes blur. 'And this is my son.'

When we leave, he takes my hands. He tells me not to forget. Never to forget. If people forget, then it will happen again.

I have always been close to the dead. Perhaps it is because I have lost so many people I love: my father, my brother, my sister. Two of my boyfriends died. Several of my friends died reporting war and two killed themselves. One put a bullet in his head, the other hanged himself.

I dream of them all, with alarming frequency. Once, in an especially poignant dream, my father was wearing wrinkled pyjamas. This was unusual because he was an impeccably groomed man. He was wandering the streets, in his pyjamas, looking lost.

You're dead, Daddy, I said. What are you doing here?

He looked hurt. 'Who told you I'm dead? I'm just in the next room.'

We are connected to the dead, like the bridges that span the Miljacka River, like the Princip Bridge on which Prince Ferdinand was shot in Sarajevo, commencing the Great War. I think sometimes we never lose the dead. I believe strongly we must never forget them. During the war, I used to read the Anne Sexton poem 'The Truth the Dead Know', over and over, as if it had a clue to the insanity that was killing the city of Sarajevo.

> *... and what of the dead? They lie without shoes*
> *in their stone boats. They are more like stone*
> *than the sea would be if it stopped. They refuse*
> *to be blessed, throat, eye and knucklebone.*

Louie was a soldier, and my friend. A tall, thin Serb from Sarajevo who fought on the Bosnian side. He was my unofficial bodyguard, a big brother, a protector. He was never a comforter – too gruff for that – but he was someone I knew I could trust with my life. He says, 'No one ever touched you during the war because of me.'

In those days, when I would fall into deep despair, out of fear or loneliness or isolation or sorrow, he would take me to strange places with strange people – gangsters, probably – where they had a bottle of whisky. Then we would smoke and drink, and he would say, 'Feel better? Now go home.' He would drive me home and walk me to my door. He never touched me, although he loved women.

When I see him now, he is so much, much older. He shakes. He drinks a lot. He carries a sadness that I know you cannot wash away, or scour clean, the way the nuns in the orphanage did.

What is it you saw? What did you taste, what did you smell? Those first days of war when you and your friends tried to hold off the tanks with Kalashnikovs, when you gathered at a factory out near the airport, a small virtually helpless band of boy Davids trying to fight off Goliath – what did you think?

Louie and I return on my last day in the new Sarajevo to all the places of the dead. To the front lines where he fought, eighteen years ago. He has never been back, and at some moments while we stare silently at the buildings where he crouched with a gun, at the factory where the battle raged for more than twenty-four hours, I am thinking perhaps it was not a good idea to bring him back.

'My nerves,' he says to me. 'Now you wonder why I shake so much?'

We stand on a railway bridge in Otes, a suburb of Sarajevo, and he looks like he will cry: we had no guns, he says quietly, we had only rifles that cost a hundred Deutschmarks and we tried to take the guns from the dead soldiers . . . We look down at a muddy, polluted creek, and I can still see the dead bodies, floating, bloated.

At the Jewish cemetery, the scene of some of the heaviest fighting, where the men fought from headstone to headstone, someone has built a new house. A sparkling *Architectural Digest* house that leans out over the city heights, with a view of Sarajevo below. It's someone who was not here during the war of course – if he was, he would not live here, among so many dead, so many lingering dead.

Then we go to Dobrinja. It was a wild place, a suburb cut off from the rest of the city for most of the war, where the fighting was always intense. I remember days of shelling, of sitting with people screaming from fear and pain, of running across fields of snow with soldiers urging me to run faster, run faster, reporter run faster . . .

In Dobrinja – where transporters opened up on the civilians on 4 May 1992 and a loudspeaker urged the people to take hand luggage and leave (not many of the population of 45,000 did), Louie fought hand to hand. He was what they called a defender of the city.

But when we go back, there is a terrible moment when neither of us can remember anything. We go back to the main street – now called Branilaca Dobrinje – Defenders of Dobrinja – but we can't recognize our old landmarks. We grope like the blind, trying to feel, trying to recall, trying to pull out of our memories what happened.

Instead of a wasted, grey outlay of Communist-style buildings eaten away by tank shells and dead faces, and people running from snipers, there are pizza parlours, a playground, gold shops, gangs of beautiful teenagers smoking cigarettes, a sports hall and dogs rolling in the early-spring sun.

'My God,' Louie says. His eyes tear up. 'I can't remember anything. I can't see where we were . . .' He climbs out of his car and lights a cigarette. He is growing agitated. He is shaking again. He stares and stares at the buildings, looking a little desperate. And I remember what I once asked my husband, who also survived many wars:

'Did this stuff, this war stuff, fuck us up?'

'How could it not?' he answered.

I can't remember anything in Dobrinja either. I can't recognize where we once stood together, in the cold, in the winter, in the summer. I can't remember the tanks. But wait – isn't that the building I sprinted from with a soldier who was taking me to the front line, holding my hand as we ran? No, it can't be. And isn't that basement the old Bosnian Army headquarters? The room where I saw that ancient woman who was dying of the cold? The place where the children were killed . . . the snow banks, the trenches, the sandbags used as defences, the metal canisters . . .

Everything has changed. Everything and nothing.

'Let's go,' Louie says quietly. 'I don't want to remember, anyway.'

As for me, I went on to report other wars, but I never fell in love with a place again. Like a first love that breaks your heart, and that's it: scarred forever.

The city on the river captivated me, held me, haunted me. One day, in a fit of madness, I burned every single notebook I reported the siege on, page by page, in a fire in a friend's garden. As the pages went up in smoke, I hoped, I thought, I was burning the worst of the memories.

But I did not. I never could.

Once upon a time, a long time ago, in a city on the river, during the month of May when there was nothing to eat but cherries that fell from the trees, I fell in love with a soldier.

He was very young – twenty-one – and still in some ways a kid. When he ran along the front lines near the river, he loped, like a wolf. He was fast, a sprinter, and before the war he was a student of journalism and politics. His eyesight was perfect, and so they gave him a gun and made him a sniper.

It was not the kind of love where you run away together and get married and have children and live happily after. It was an unconsummated love between two people who had fallen through the rabbit hole and gone mad with war, drunk with war. We lived together in an apartment on a front line so vicious that we heard the shells crashing and throbbing, sometimes it was so insane that I thought I heard him laughing and laughing. But later he told me he was crying.

Years later we meet in the new, spanking clean Hotel Europa. He is not a boy. He has a good job and wears a suit. After the war, he spent years abroad, trying to forget. He is a father, I am a mother.

When we hug each other, it is the touching of two strange survivors. But we have the same DNA. On 11 September 2001, he found me somehow, and rang me on my cellphone – I was in Paris getting a visa to go to Afghanistan – and said: I love you.

On my last day in Sarajevo, I tell him about Nusrat. I ask him to look out for him, a beggar in the parking lot who is only twenty-seven but will look a hundred. He promises he will try, though he warns me that perhaps Nusrat does not want to be found. But Jasna wanted to be found, and Alija wanted to be found, I say. Sometimes people want to remember.

He orders another beer and lights a cigarette.

'No. They want to forget.' Every war drowns out another, he tells me. Rwanda drowned out Bosnia. Somalia drowned out Rwanda.

Sierra Leone drowned out Somalia, Iraq drowned out Israel, Afghanistan drowned out Iraq . . . and so on and so on until no one remembers anything.

Later, I ask him what happened to this city. Why did the people rip each other to pieces? Everyone calls it an ethnic war, or a religious war, but it was neither. It was about politics, greed, land-grabbing, and how it can eat you up, turn you crazy, make you turn on your neighbour. It was about politicians and power.

You should let it go, he says, finally.

He looks distant. He looks remote. He says nothing. He gets up to take his long, black coat. I want to cry, but I don't.

He cups my face in his hands. He kisses me goodbye. He goes through the door of the Hotel Europa, into the new world, perhaps even more frightening than the comfortable world of the war, and I know he is forgetting and remembering. ■

Don't Flinch

Lichen-green lines of shingle pulsate and waver
when you lift your eyes. It's the glare. Don't flinch
The news you were reading
(who tramples whom) is antique
and on the death pages you've seen already
worms doing their normal work
on the life that was: the chewers chewing
at a sensuality that wrestled doom
an anger steeped in love they can't
even taste. How could this still
shock or sicken you? Friends go missing, mute
nameless. Toss
the paper. Reach again
for the *Iliad*. The lines
pulse into sense. Turn up the music
Now do you hear it? can you smell smoke
under the near shingles?

DYKE BRIDGE

Peter Orner

Chappaquiddick, Massachusetts, 1976

My brother and I in the knee-deep water, standing in the tidal current, under Dyke Bridge. We are hunting whelks. Yes, it is the water Mary Jo Kopechne drowned in. I know all about it. About Teddy drunk and how the story of what happened was less covered up than simply muddled. My brother tells me all about it. How Teddy was still grieving his brothers, both his shot-to-death brothers, and that maybe he drank too much. Not that this excuses what happened, my brother says. *But wouldn't you drink if somebody shot me in the head? And then your other brother? If you had another brother? Wouldn't you drink a whole hell of a lot and probably crash a car?*

We are on vacation with our parents on Martha's Vineyard. We are from Illinois. It is classy if you are from Illinois to take a vacation on Martha's Vineyard. And Kennedyesque. My parents are still married (to each other), although my brother and I would prefer this not to be the case. We have ridden our bikes out to this bridge to see this very spot, to muck around in this famous water. My brother is wearing a T-shirt with the face of Sam Ervin, the hero of Watergate, on it.

I want to remember that we were alone, that it was only the two of us, but somewhere, in some stack of pictures, in some cabinet in my father's house, there are pictures of the two of us standing under Dyke Bridge, so it must be that at least one of our parents was with us and recorded it, and since my mother rarely took pictures it had to have been my father; but let's leave him out of this. Just my brother and me in the knee-deep water and my brother telling me that Teddy was heading back to the island that night, back from the even smaller island where there'd been a party. That he was driving a black Chevrolet, because the Kennedys may be richer than God but they aren't ostentatious. When you're that rich you don't drive a Mercedes. And that Mary Jo Kopechne wasn't even very beautiful. She wasn't Teddy's wife either, he says, but that goes with this territory.

What territory?

The territory of being richer than God, my brother says. The landscape of sex and whisperings and innuendo.

I would rather fish up a whelk than listen to this, a live whelk with the black body inside, a Jell-O-ish squirmy thing that we will take back to our rented house and boil alive on the stove.

Even so, I ask, how much not very beautiful was she?

And my brother says, not particularly unbeautiful. Just not that beautiful for a Kennedy. She wasn't Jackie, is what I'm trying to say. But anyway, nobody was Jackie. But still, Teddy may have even loved her even though he hardly knew her. Especially after she suffocated to death.

What do you mean?

My brother stares at me for a while. He and I have the same eyes, which is sometimes creepy. You don't know yourself coming and going, as my grandmother used to say. Then he squats in the water and takes up a couple of handfuls of ocean water and raises his hands to his nose as if to smell the water as it flows through his fingers. Don't we kind of love what we kill? my brother says. What about the whelks?

Our bikes are on the bridge, leaning against a broken piling. Dyke Bridge is a tiny bridge, a miniature bridge. It is not much bigger than the width of a Chevy and nearly the same length. Driving off it is the bathroom equivalent of falling out of the bathtub.

I email my brother and ask him if he remembers all this. He writes back and says he doesn't remember it that way. And he is still very sensitive when it comes to the Kennedys. Like my mother, he remains a staunch believer in the notion that the New England wisdom embodied by the Kennedys will save this doomed country yet. My brother works for a congressman in Washington.

The bridge is bigger than a bathtub. Why do you have to exaggerate? Isn't the truth bad enough? You think Teddy Kennedy doesn't curse his soul every day for that night? Leave the man alone, even in your lying memories. I remember. We were out there with Dad. He took pictures. He thought it was funny. He kept saying be careful not to step on Mary Jo's face. You were annoyed because he kept saying you had to hold still for the picture.

And furthermore, my brother says, I should not, even over private electronic communication (*remember, don't use my .gov account for things like this*), provide aid and succour to the haters who still love to dredge this story up out of the muck. Remember Chappaquiddick! Besides, he says, why don't you ever just pick up the phone and call me? Why do you email your brother? It gives the illusion of distance, I tell him. Pretend I'm in Shanghai or somewhere.

He replies: *Anyway, isn't anything drive-offable if you put your mind to it? Or even when you don't, especially when you don't? You're gonna pass judgement? Look at your own life.*

My brother is right. He is right. Even when he is not right he is right. Look at my own life. And nothing he has ever told me have I forgotten.

It is only that something happened there, under that bridge, where my brother and I once swam. As things do, as they always have, so many more things (strange things, impossible things) than we can even imagine. Dream it up and chances are it already happened. One minute you're drunk and laughing and your hand is on her bare thigh and the next hood of the car is in the sand and water's flowing in through the cracks in the windows and the car's like a big fat grounded fish and there's this woman – what is her name? – flailing her arms in the darkness and shouting and you wonder for a moment if you love her. What was her name again? I'm confused. This is all so much black confusion. Shouldn't I be swimmingly noble? Don't I know the cross-chest carry? Aren't I a Kennedy? Aren't I the brother of the hero of PT-109? Isn't now the time? No. Now is not the time. Now is the time to save yourself. Doesn't matter who you are (or your brothers are), Senator, save yourself – and then run. Everybody runs. My brother once said (though he doesn't remember): Don't we sort of love what we kill? Maybe it's even true. But before that you got to run like hell. This I've learned on my own. There'll always be time for nobility, honour, sorrow, remorse, yes, maybe even love – in the morning.

The shadow from that little bridge over our heads. Us in the dark water, my brother and me, in the gummy sand, July 1976. ■

LITQUAKE
SAN FRANCISCO'S LITERARY FESTIVAL

SEE   HEAR   SPEAK

San Francisco
OCTOBER 1-9

litquake.org

New York
SEPTEMBER 11

litcrawl.org

"Hipsters, word nerds and wordsmiths crawl out from behind their books and computers to mingle" -- San Francisco Chronicle

'...ull of useful stuff. It answered ...
...very question' – J.K. ROWLIN...

www.writersandartists.co.uk

'Practical, no-nonsense, supportive and encouraging –
quite simply the best friend an aspiring writer can have'
Julie Myerson

Writers' & Artists' YEARBOOK 2011

THE No1 BESTSELLER
Completely revised and updated every year

2011

Writers' & Artists' YEARBOOK

A&C B

...RITERS AND ARTISTS FOR OVER 1...
...sential reading ... how to survi...
...n publishing' – KATE MOSSE

...OUS ABOUT GETTING PUBLISHE...
...advice and feedback from industry specia...
...ne of our writing conferences or mastercl...
...nformation, visit: www.writersandartists...

...ww.writersandartists.co.uk

CEILING

Chimamanda Ngozi Adichie

When Obinze first saw her email, he was sitting in the back of his Land Rover in still Lagos traffic, his jacket slung over the front seat, a rusty-haired child beggar glued to his window, a hawker pressing colourful CDs against the other window, the radio turned on low to the pidgin English news on Wazobia FM, and the grey gloom of imminent rain all around. He stared at his BlackBerry, his body suddenly rigid. First, he skimmed the email, dampened that it was not longer. *Ceiling, kedu? I saw Amaka yesterday in New York and she said you were doing well with work, wife – and a child! Proud Papa. Congratulations. I'm still teaching and doing some research, but seriously thinking of moving back to Nigeria soon. Let's keep in touch? Ifemelu.*

He read it again slowly and felt the urge to smooth something, his trousers, his shaved-bald head. She had called him Ceiling. In the last email from her, sent just before he got married four years ago, she had called him Obinze, wished him happiness in breezy sentences, and mentioned the Black American she was living with. A gracious email. He had hated it. He had hated it so much that he googled the Black American, a lecturer at Yale, and found it infuriating that she lived with a man who referred on his blog to friends as 'cats', but it was the photo of the Black American, oozing intellectual cool in distressed jeans and black-framed eyeglasses, that had tipped Obinze over, made him send her a cold reply. *Thank you for the good wishes, I have never been happier in my life*, he'd written. It was complete bullshit, stupid posturing, and she had to recognize this; nobody knew him as well as she did. He hoped she would write something mocking back – so unlike her, not to have been even vaguely tart – but she did not write at all and when he emailed her again, after his honeymoon in Morocco, to say he wanted to keep in touch and wanted to talk sometime, she did not reply.

The traffic was moving. A light rain was falling. The child beggar ran along, his doe-eyed expression more theatrical, his motions frantic: bringing his hand to his mouth, over and over, fingertips pursed together. Obinze rolled down the window and held out a hundred-naira note. His driver Gabriel watched with grave disapproval from the rear-view mirror.

'God bless you, *oga!*' the child beggar said.

'Don't be giving money to these beggars, sir,' Gabriel said. 'They are all rich. They are using begging to make big money in this Lagos. I heard about one that built a block of six flats in Ikeja!'

'So why are you working as a driver instead of a beggar, Gabriel?' Obinze asked and laughed, a little too heartily. He wanted to tell Gabriel that his girlfriend from university had just emailed him, actually his girlfriend from university *and* secondary school. The first time she let him take off her bra, she lay on her back moaning softly, her hands on his head, and afterwards she said, 'My eyes were open but I did not see the ceiling. This never happened before.' She was seventeen and he was eighteen and other girls would have pretended that they had never let another boy touch them, but not her, never her. There was a vivid honesty about her, which he had found so disconcerting and then so irresistible. *Longing for ceiling, can't wait for my period to end,* she once wrote on the back of his notebook during a lecture. Then, later, she began to call him Ceiling, in a playful way, in a suggestive way – but when they fought or when she retreated into moodiness, she called him Obinze. 'Why do you call him Ceiling anyway?' his friend Chidi once asked her, on one of those languorous days after first-semester exams. She had joined a group of his classmates sitting around a filthy plastic table in a beer parlour outside campus. She drank from her bottle of Maltina, swallowed, glanced at him and said, 'Because he is so tall his head touches the ceiling, can't you see?' Her deliberate slowness, the small smile that stretched her lips, made it clear that she wanted them to know that this was not why she called him Ceiling. And he was not tall. She kicked him under the table and he kicked her back, watching his laughing friends; they were all a little afraid of her and a little in love with her. Did she see the ceiling when the

Black American touched her? Had she used ceiling with other men? It upset him now to think that she might have. His phone rang and for a hopeful, confused moment he thought it was Ifemelu calling from America.

'Darling, *kedu ebe I no?*' His wife, Kosi, always began her calls to him with those words: where are you? He never asked where she was when he called her, but she would tell him anyway: I'm just getting to the salon. I'm on Third Mainland Bridge. It was as if she needed the reassurance of their concrete physicality when they were not together. She had a high, girlish voice. They were supposed to be at Chief's house for the party at 7.30 p.m. and it was already past six.

He told her he was in traffic. 'But it's moving, and we've just turned into Ozumba Mbadiwe. I'm coming.'

On Lekki Expressway the traffic moved swiftly in the waning rain and soon Gabriel was sounding the horn in front of the high black gates of his home. Mohammed, the gateman, wiry in his dirty white kaftan, flung open the gates and raised a hand in greeting. Obinze looked at the yellow colonnaded house. Inside was his furniture, imported from Italy, his wife, his two-year-old daughter, Buchi, the nanny Christiana, his wife's sister Chioma who was on a forced holiday because university lecturers were on strike yet again, and the new housegirl Marie who had been brought from Benin Republic after his wife decided that Nigerian housegirls were unsuitable. There would be the smell of cooking, the television downstairs would be showing a film on the Africa Magic channel and, pervading it all, the still air of well-being. He climbed out of the car. His gait was stiff, his legs difficult to lift. He had begun, in the past months, to feel bloated from all he had acquired – the family, the house, the other properties in Ikoyi and Abuja, the cars, the bank accounts in Dubai and London – and he would be overcome by the urge to prick everything with a pin, to deflate it all, to be free. He was no longer sure, he had in fact never been sure, whether he liked his life because he really did or whether he liked it because he was supposed to.

'Darling,' Kosi said, opening the door before he got to it.

Her dress was cinched at the waist and made her figure look very hour-glassy.

'Daddy-daddy!' Buchi said.

He swung her up and then hugged his wife, carefully avoiding her lips, painted pink and lined in a darker pink. 'You look beautiful, babe,' he said. '*Asa! Ugo!*'

She laughed. The same way she laughed, with an open, accepting enjoyment, when people asked her, 'Is your mother white? Are you a half-caste?' because she was so fair-skinned. It had always discomfited him, the pleasure she took in being mistaken for mixed-race.

'Will you bathe or just change? I brought out your new blue kaftan. I knew you'd want to wear traditional,' she said, following him upstairs. 'Do you want to eat before we go? You know Chief will have nice food.'

'I'll just change and we can go,' he said.

He was tired. It was not a physical fatigue – he used his treadmill regularly and felt better than he had in years – but a draining lassitude that numbed the margins of his mind. He went out every day, he made money, he came home, he played with his daughter, he watched television, he ate, he read books, he slept with his wife. He did things because he did them.

Chief's party would bore him, as usual, but he went because he went to all of Chief's parties and perhaps because Kosi liked going. She enjoyed being surrounded by glittery people, hugging women she barely knew, calling the older ones Ma with exaggerated respect, soaking up their compliments, dispensing hers, basking in being so beautiful but flattening her personality so that her beauty was non-threatening. He had always been struck by this, how important it was to her to be a wholesomely agreeable person, to have no sharp angles sticking out. On Sundays, she would invite his relatives for pounded yam and *onugbu* soup and then watch over to make sure everyone was suitably overfed. *Uncle, you must eat oh! There is more meat in the kitchen! Let me bring you another Guinness!* When they visited his mother's house in Enugu, she always flew up to help with serving the food, and when his mother made to clean up afterwards, she would get up, offended, and say, 'Mummy, how can I be here and you will be cleaning?' She ended every sentence she spoke to his uncles with 'sir'. She put ribbons in the hair of his cousins' daughters. There was something immodest about her modesty: it announced itself.

At the party, he watched her, gold shimmer on her eyelids, as she greeted Mrs Akin-Cole, curtsying and smiling, and he thought about the day their baby, slippery, curly-haired Buchi, was born at the Portland Hospital in London, how she had turned to him while he was still fiddling with his latex gloves and said, with something like apology, 'We'll have a boy next time.' He had recoiled. What he felt for her then was a gentle contempt, for not knowing that he was indifferent about the gender of their child, for assuming that he would want a boy since most men wanted a boy. Perhaps he should have talked more with her, about the baby they were expecting and about everything else, because although they exchanged pleasant sounds and were good friends and shared comfortable silences, they did not really talk. Her world view was a set of conventional options that she mulled over while he did not even consider any of those options; the questions he asked of life were entirely different from hers. Of course he knew this from the beginning, had sensed it in their first conversation after his friend Chidi introduced them at a wedding. She was wearing a lime-green bridesmaid's dress in satin, cut low to show a cleavage he could not stop looking at, and somebody was making a speech, describing the bride as 'a woman of virtue' and Kosi nodded eagerly and whispered to him, 'She is a true woman of virtue.' Even then he had felt gentle contempt that she could use the word 'virtue' without the slightest irony, as was done in the badly written articles in the women's section of the weekend newspapers. Still, he had wanted her, chased her with a lavish single-mindedness. He had never seen a woman with such a perfect incline to her cheekbones, that made her entire face seem so alive in an architectural way, lifting when she smiled, and he was newly disorientated from his quick wealth: one week, he was squatting in his cousin's flat and sleeping on a thin mattress on the floor and the next he owned a house and two cars. He felt as if his life was no longer his. It was Kosi who made it start to seem believable. She moved into his new house from her hostel at the University of Lagos and arranged her perfume bottles on his dresser, citrusy scents that he came to associate with home, and she sat in the BMW beside him as though it had always been his car, and when they showered together, she scrubbed him with a rough sponge, even between his toes, until he felt reborn. Until he owned his new life. A year passed before she told him her relatives were asking what his intentions were. 'They just keep asking,' she said and stressed the 'they' to exclude herself from the marriage clamour. He recognized, and disliked, her manipulation. (The same way he felt when, after months of trying to get pregnant, she began to say with sulky righteousness, 'All my friends who lived very rough lives are pregnant'.) Still, he married her. Perhaps he was already on autopilot then. He felt an obligation to do so, he was not unhappy, and he imagined that she would, with time, gain a certain heft. She had not, after almost five years, except physically, in a way that he thought made her look even more beautiful, fresher, with fuller hips and breasts, like a well-watered house plant.

Watching her now as she talked to Mrs Akin-Cole, he felt guilty about his thoughts. She was such a devoted woman, such a well-meaning, devoted woman. He reached out and held her hand. She often told him that her friends envied her, and said he behaved like a foreign husband, the way he took her to all his social events, made her breakfast on Sundays, stayed home every night.

Mrs Akin-Cole was talking about sending Buchi to the French school. 'They are very good, very rigorous. Of course, they teach in French but it can only be good for the child to learn another civilized language, since she already learns English at home.'

'OK, Auntie. I'll go there and talk to them,' Kosi said. 'I know I have to start early.'

'The French school is not bad but I prefer Meadowland. They teach the complete British curriculum,' the other woman, whose name Obinze had forgotten but who had made a lot of money during General Abacha's military government, said. The story was that she had been a pimp of some sort, providing women for army officers and getting inflated supply contracts in exchange.

'Oh, yes. Meadowland. I'll look at that one, too,' Kosi said.

'Why?' Obinze asked. 'Didn't we all go to primary schools that taught the Nigerian curriculum?'

The women looked at him.

Finally, Mrs Akin-Cole said, 'But things have changed, my dear Obinze,' and shook her head pitifully, as though he was an adolescent.

'I agree,' Kosi said and Obinze wanted to ask what the fuck it was she agreed with anyway.

'If you decide to disadvantage your child by sending her to one of these schools with half-baked Nigerian teachers . . .' Mrs Akin-Cole shrugged. She spoke with that unplaceable foreign accent, British and American and something else all at once, of the wealthy Nigerian who did not want the world to forget how worldly she was, how her British Airways executive card was choking with miles.

'One of my friends sent her child to St Mary's and do you know, they have only five computers in the whole school. Only five!' the other woman said.

'We'll go to the British school and French school,' Kosi said and looked at him with a plea. He shrugged. He would ordinarily not have said anything at all to Mrs Akin-Cole but today he wanted to pluck the sneer from her face and crumple it and hurl it back. But Chief was upon them.

'Princess!' Chief said to Kosi and hugged her, pressing her close; Obinze wondered if Chief had propositioned her in the past. It would not surprise him. He had once been at Chief's house when a man brought his girlfriend to visit, and when she left the room to go to the toilet, Obinze heard Chief tell the man, 'I like that girl. Give her to me and I will give you a nice plot in Victoria Island.'

'You look so well, Chief,' Kosi said. 'Ever young!'

'Ah, my dear, I try, I try.' Chief jokingly tugged at the satin lapels of his black jacket. He did look well, spare and upright unlike many of his peers in their sixties. 'My boy!' he said to Obinze.

'Good evening, Chief.' Obinze shook him with both hands, bowing slightly. He watched the other men at the party bow, too, crowding around Chief, jostling to out-laugh one another when Chief made a joke. They were all men who wore conspicuous watches, who had loud conversations about the things they owned, the sort of men that *City People* referred to as 'Lagos Big Boys'. They reminded Obinze of the three men he saw in Chief's house the first day his cousin took him there. They had been in the living room sipping cognac while Chief pontificated about politics. 'Exactly! Correct! Thank you! You have just nailed the exact problem, Chief!' they crowed from time to time. Obinze had watched, fascinated. He was only a month in Lagos after being deported from England, but his cousin Amaka had started to grumble about how he could not just stay in her flat reading and moping, how he was not the first person to be deported, after all, and how he needed to hustle. Lagos was about hustling. His mates were hustling. She was Chief's girlfriend – *he has many but I am one of the serious ones; he doesn't buy cars for everyone,* she said – and so she brought him to Chief's house to introduce them and see if Chief would help him. Chief was a difficult man, she told him, and it was important to catch him in a good mood when he was at his most expansive. They had, apparently, because after the three men left, Chief turned to Obinze and asked, 'Do you know that song "No One Knows Tomorrow"?' Then he proceeded to sing the song with childish gusto. *No one knows tomorrow! To-mo-rrow! No one knows tomorrow!* Another generous splash of cognac in his glass. 'That is the principle on which the ambitious segment of the Nigerian society is based. No one knows tomorrow. Look at those big bankers with all their money and the next thing they knew, they were in prison. Look at that pauper who could not pay his rent yesterday and now because Babangida gave him an oil well, he has a private jet!'

Chief always spoke with a triumphant tone, mundane observations delivered as grand discoveries. After Obinze had visited a few more times, drawn in part because Chief's steward always served fresh pepper soup, and because Amaka told him to just keep hanging around until Chief did something for him, Chief told him, 'You are hungry and honest, that is very rare in this country. Is that not so?'

'Yes,' Obinze said, even though he was not sure whether he was agreeing about his own quality or the rarity of it.

'Everybody is hungry, even the rich men are hungry, but nobody is honest. Twenty years ago I had nothing until somebody introduced me to General Babangida's brother. He saw that I was hungry and honest and he gave me some contacts. Look at me today. I have money. Even my great-grandchildren will not finish eating my money. But power? Yes, that one I work hard to have. I was Babangida's friend. I was Abacha's friend. Now that the military has gone, Obasanjo is my friend. The man has created opportunities in this country. Big opportunities for people like me. I know they are going to privatize the National Farm Support Corporation because they said it is bankrupt. Do you know this? No. By the time you know it, I would have taken a position and I would have benefited from the arbitrage. That is our free market!' Chief laughed. 'The Corporation was set up in the 1960s and it owns property everywhere. The houses are all rotten and termites are eating the roofs. But they are selling them. I'm going to buy seven properties for five million each. You know what they are listed for in the books? One million. You know what the real worth is? Fifty million.' Chief stopped again to laugh and swallow some cognac. 'So I will put you in charge of that deal. They need somebody to do the evaluation consulting and I will put you there. Amaka said you are sharp and I can see it in your face. Your first job will be to help me make money but your second job will be to make your own money. You will make sure you undervalue the properties and make sure it looks as if we are all following due process. It's not difficult. You acquire the property, sell off half to pay your purchase price and you are in business! You'll build a house in Lekki and buy some cars and ask your home town to give you some titles and your friends to put congratulatory messages in the newspapers for you and before you know, any bank you walk into, they will want to package a loan immediately and give you, because they think you no longer need the money. Ah, Nigeria! No one knows tomorrow!' Chief paused to stare at one of his ringing cellphones – four were placed on the table next to him – and then ignored it and leaned back on his leather sofa. 'And after you register your own company, you must find a white man. You had friends in England before you were deported? Find one white man. Tell everybody he is your general manager. It gives you immediate legitimacy with many idiots in this country. This is how Nigeria works, I'm telling you.'

And it was, indeed, how it worked and still worked for Obinze. The ease of it had disorientated him. The first time he took his offer letter to the bank, he had felt surreal saying 'fifty' and 'fifty-five' and leaving out the 'million' because there was no need to state the obvious. That day, he had written an email to Ifemelu, which was still in the drafts folder of his old Hotmail account, unsent after six years. She was the only person who would understand and yet he was afraid that she would feel contempt for the person he had become. He still did not understand why Chief had decided to help him; there was, after all, a trail of eager visitors to Chief's house, people bringing relatives and friends, all of them with pleas in their eyes. He sometimes wondered if Chief would one day ask something of him, the hungry and honest boy he had groomed, and in his more melodramatic moments, he imagined Chief asking him to organize an assassination.

The party was more crowded, suffocating. Chief was saying something to a group of men and Obinze heard the end: 'But you know that as we speak, oil is flowing through illegal pipes and they sell it in bottles in Cotonou!' He was distracted. He reached into his pocket to touch his BlackBerry. Kosi was asking if he wanted more food. He didn't. He wanted to go home. A rash eagerness had overcome him, to go into his study and reply to Ifemelu's email, something he had unconsciously been composing in his mind. If she was considering coming back to Nigeria then it meant she was no longer with the Black American. But she might be bringing him with her; she was, after all, the kind of woman who would make a man easily uproot his life, the kind who, because she did not expect certainty, made a certain kind of sureness somehow become possible. When she held his hand during those campus days, she would squeeze until both palms became slick with sweat, and each time she would say, 'Just in case this is the last time we hold hands, let's really hold hands. Because a motorcycle or a car can kill us now, or I might see the real man of my dreams down the street and leave you, or you might see the real woman of your dreams and leave me.'

Perhaps the Black American would come back to Nigeria too, clinging on to her. Still, there was something about the email that made him feel she was single. He brought out his BlackBerry to calculate the American time when it had been sent. In the car on the way home, Kosi asked what was wrong. He pretended not to have heard and asked Gabriel to turn off the radio and put in a Fela CD. He had introduced Ifemelu to Fela at university. She had, before then, thought of Fela as the mad weed-smoker who wore only underwear while performing, but she had come to love the Afro-beat sound and they would lie on his mattress and listen to it and then she would leap up and make swift, slightly vulgar movements with her hips when the run-run-run chorus came on. He wondered if she remembered that. Kosi was asking again what was wrong.

'Nothing,' he said.

'You didn't eat very much,' she said.

'Too much pepper in the rice.'

'Darling, you didn't even eat the rice. Was it Mrs Akin-Cole?'

He shrugged and told her he was thinking about the new block of flats he had just completed in Parkview. He hoped Shell would rent it because the oil companies were always the best renters, never complaining about abrupt hikes, paying easily in American dollars so that nobody had to deal with the fluctuating naira.

'Don't worry. God will bring Shell. We will be OK, darling,' she said and touched his shoulder.

The flats were in fact already rented by an oil company but he sometimes told her senseless lies such as this, because a part of him hoped she would ask a question or challenge him about something, but he knew she would not, because all she wanted was to make sure the conditions of their life remained the same, and how he made that happen she left entirely to him. She had never asked him about his time in England either. Of course she knew that he was deported, but she had never asked him for details. He was no longer sure that he wanted her to, or even whether he would have told her about feeling invisible in that removal centre, but it suddenly became a glaring failing of hers. Ifemelu would have asked. Ifemelu would not have been content to ignore the past as long as the present existed. He knew very well what he was doing, fashioning a perfect doll from ten-year-old memories of Ifemelu, but he could not help himself.

At home, the housegirl Marie opened the door and Kosi said, 'Please make food for your *oga*.'

'Yes, ma.'

She was slight and Obinze was not sure whether she was timid or whether her not speaking English well made her seem so. She had been with them only a month. The last housegirl, brought by a relative of Gabriel's, was stocky and had arrived clutching a duffel bag. He was not there when Kosi looked through it – she did that routinely with all domestic help because she wanted to know what was being brought into her home – but he came out when he heard Kosi shouting. He stood by the door and watched her, holding two packets of condoms by their very tips, swinging them in the air. 'What is this for? Eh? You came to my house to be a prostitute?'

The girl looked down at first, silent, then she looked Kosi in the face and said quietly, 'In my last job, my madam's husband was always harassing me, forcing me.'

Kosi's eyes bulged. She moved forward for a moment, as though to attack the girl in some way, and then stopped.

'Please carry your bag and go now-now,' she said.

The girl shifted, looking a little surprised, and then she picked up her bag and turned to the door. After she left, Kosi said, 'Can you believe the nonsense? She brought condoms to my house and she opened her mouth to say that rubbish. Can you believe it?'

'Her former employer raped her so she decided to protect herself this time,' Obinze said.

Kosi stared at him. 'You feel sorry for her. You don't know these housegirls. How can you feel sorry for her?'

He wanted to ask, '*How can you not?*' But the tentative fear in her eyes silenced him. Her insecurity was so great and so ordinary. She was not worried about his lassitude, or about their not having real conversations, or indeed about their not truly knowing each other. Instead she was worried about a housegirl whom it would never even occur to him to seduce. It was not as if he did not know what living in Lagos could do to a woman married to a young and wealthy man, how easy it was to slip into paranoia about 'Lagos girls', those sophisticated monsters of glamour who swallowed husbands whole, slithering them down their throats. But he wished she handled her fear a little differently, pushed back a little more. Once he had told her about the attractive banker who had come to his office to talk to him about opening an account. He had found it amusing and sad, how desperate the woman had been, in her tight pencil skirt and fitted shirt with one button that should not have been open, trying to pretend that she was in control of it all. Kosi had not been amused. 'I know Lagos girls, she can do anything,' she had said, and what had struck him was that Kosi seemed no longer to see him, Obinze, and instead she saw blurred figures who were types: a wealthy man, a female banker who had been given a target amount to bring in as deposits, an easy exchange.

She had, in the years since they got married, developed an inordinate dislike of single women and an inordinate love of God. Before they got married, she went to Sunday Mass once a week at the Catholic Church but afterwards, she had thrown her rosary in the dustbin and told him she would now go to the House of David because it was a Bible-believing and spirit-filled church. Later, when he found out that House of David had a special prayer service for Keeping Your Husband, he had been flattered and revolted. Just as he was when he once asked why her best friend from university, Elohor, hardly visited them, and Kosi said, 'She's still single,' as though that was a self-evident reason.

Marie knocked on his study door and came in with a tray of rice and fried plantains. He ate slowly. He thought of the day he was frying plantains for Ifemelu in the tiny room he rented on campus, how he had insisted on washing the plantain slices even though she had asked him not to, and how hot oil from the pan came flying out and left ovals of burned skin on his neck. Perhaps he should include this memory in the email. *Remember the fried plantain accident?* He decided not to. It would be too odd, too much a specific memory. He wrote and rewrote the email, deliberately not mentioning his wife or using the first-person plural, trying for a balance between earnest and funny. He did not want to alienate her. He wanted to make sure she would reply this time. It was alarming to him how happy that email had made him, how his mind had become busy with her, possessed by her. He clicked 'send' and then minutes later checked to see if she had replied. What was this? Was he unhappy? It was not that he was unhappy, he told himself, it was simply that he had been long enough in his new life that he had begun to think of alternative lives, people he might have become, and doors he had not opened. He got up and went out to the veranda; the sudden hot air, the roar of his neighbour's generator, the smell of diesel exhaust fumes brought a lightness to his head. Frantic winged insects flitted around the electric bulb. He felt, looking out at the muggy darkness farther away, as if he could float, and all he needed was to let himself go. ■

THE LAST THING
WE NEED

Claire Vaye Watkins

Dear Mr Moser

On the afternoon of June 25 while on my last outing to Rhyolite, I was driving down Cane Springs Road some ten miles outside Beatty and happened upon what looked to be the debris left over from an auto accident. I got out of my truck and took a look around. The valley was bone dry. A hot west wind took the puffs of dust from where I stepped and curled them away like ashes. Near the wash I found broken glass, deep gouges in the dirt running off the side of the road, and an array of freshly bought groceries tumbled among the creosote. Coke cans (some full, some open and empty, some still sealed but dented and half full and leaking). Bud Light cans in the same shape as the Coke. Fritos. Meat. Et cetera. Of particular interest to me were the two almost-full prescriptions that had been filled at the pharmacy in Tonopah only three days before, and a sealed Ziploc bag full of letters signed M. I also took notice of a bundle of photos of an old car, part primer, part rust, that I presume was or is going to be restored. The car was a Chevy Chevelle, a '66, I believe. I once knew a man who drove a Chevelle. Both medications had bright yellow stickers on their sides warning against drinking alcohol while taking them. Enter the Bud Light, and the gouges in the dirt, possibly. I copied your address off those prescription bottles. What happened out there? Where is your car? Why were the medications, food and other supplies left behind? Who are you, Duane Moser? What were you looking for out at Rhyolite?

I hope this letter finds you, and finds you well. Please write back.

Truly,
Thomas Grey
PO Box 129, Verdi
Nevada 89439

PS I left most of the debris in the desert, save for the medications, pictures and letters from M. I also took the plastic grocery bags, which I untangled from the bushes and recycled on my way through Reno. It didn't feel right to just leave them out there.

August 16
Duane Moser
1077 Pincay Drive
Henderson, Nevada 89015

Dear Mr Moser

This morning, as I fed the horses, clouds were just beginning to slide down the slope of the Sierras, and I was reminded once again of Rhyolite. When I came inside I borrowed my father's old copy of the *Physician's Desk Reference* from his room. From that book I have gathered that before driving out to Rhyolite you may have been feeling out of control, alone, or hopeless. You were possibly in a state of extreme depression; perhaps you were even considering hurting yourself. Judging by the date the prescriptions were filled and the number of pills left in the bottles – which I have counted, sitting out in the fields atop a tractor which I let sputter and die, eating the sandwich which my wife fixed me for lunch – you had not been taking the medications long enough for them to counteract your possible feelings of despair. 'Despair', 'depression', 'hopeless', 'alone'. These are the words of the *PDR*, 41st Edition, which I returned to my father promptly, as per his request. My father can be difficult. He spends his days shut up in his room, reading old crime novels populated by dames and Negroes, or watching the TV we bought him with the volume up too high. Some days he refuses to eat. Duane Moser, my father never thought he would live this long.

I think there will be lightning tonight; the air has that feel. Please, write back.

Truly,
Thomas Grey
PO Box 129, Verdi
Nevada 89439

September 1
Duane Moser
1077 Pincay Drive
Henderson, Nevada 89015

Dear Mr Moser

I slept terribly last night, dreamed dreams not easily identified as such. Had I told my wife about them she might have given me a small quartz crystal or amethyst and insisted I carry it around in my pocket all day, to cleanse my mind and spirit. She comes from California. Here is a story she likes to tell. On one of our first dates we walked arm in arm around downtown Reno, where she was a clerk at a grocery store and I was a student of agriculture and business. There she tried to pull me down a little flight of steps to the red-lit underground residence of a palm reader and psychic. I declined. Damn near an hour she pulled on me, saying what was I afraid of, asking what was the big deal. I am not a religious man but, as I told her then, there are some things I'd rather not fuck with. Now she likes to say it's a good thing I wouldn't go in because if that psychic had told her that she'd be stuck with me for going on fourteen years now she would have turned and headed for the hills. Ha! And I say, Honey, not as fast as I would've, ha, ha! This is our old joke. Like all our memories, we like to take it out once in a while and lay it flat on the kitchen table, the way my wife does with her sewing patterns, where we line up the shape of our life against that which we thought it would be by now.

I'll tell you what I don't tell her, that there is something shameful in this, the buoying of our sinking spirits with old stories.

I imagine you a man alone, Duane Moser, with no one asking after your dreams in the morning, no one slipping healing rocks into your pockets. A bachelor. It was the Fritos, finally, which reminded me of the gas station in Beatty where I worked when I was in high school and where I knew a man who owned a Chevelle like yours, a '66. But it occurs to me perhaps this assumption is foolish; surely there are wives out there who have not banned trans fats and processed sugars, as mine has. I haven't had a Frito in eleven years. Regardless, I write to enquire about your family, should you reply.

Our children came to us later in life than most. My oldest, Danielle, has just started school. Her little sister, Layla, is having a hard time with it. She wants so badly to go to school with Danielle that she screams and cries as the school bus pulls away in the morning. Sometimes she throws herself down to the ground, embedding little pieces of rock in the flesh of her fists. Then she is sullen and forlorn for the rest of the day. My wife worries for her, but truth be told, I am encouraged. The sooner Layla understands that we are nothing but the sum of that which we endure, the better. But my father has taken to walking Layla to the end of our gravel road in the afternoon to wait for Danielle at the bus stop. Layla likes to go as early as she is allowed, as if her being there will bring the bus sooner. She would stand at the end of the road all day if we let her. She pesters my father so that he sometimes stands there in the heat with her for an hour or more, though his heart is in no condition to be doing so. In many ways he is better to my girls than I am. He is far better to them than he was to me. I am not a religious man but I do thank God for that.

I am beginning to think I dreamed you up. Please, write soon.

Truly,
Thomas Grey
PO Box 129, Verdi
Nevada 89439

October 16
Duane Moser
1077 Pincay Drive
Henderson, Nevada 89015

Dear Mr Moser

I have read the letters from M, the ones you kept folded in the Ziploc bag. Forgive me, but for all I know you may be dead, and I could not resist. I read them in my shed, where the stink and thickness of the air were almost unbearable, and then again in my truck in the parking lot of the Verdi post office. I was struck, as I was when I first found them out near Rhyolite on Cane Springs Road, by how new the letters looked. Though most were written nearly twenty years ago the paper is clean, the creases sharp. Duane Moser, what I do not understand is this: why a Ziploc bag? Did you worry they might get wet on your journey through the desert in the middle of summer? Then again, I am reminded of the Coke and Bud Light. Or am I to take the Ziploc bag as an indication of your fierce, protective love for M.? Is it a sign, as M. suggests, that little by little you sealed your whole self off, until there was nothing left for her? Furthermore, I have to ask whether you committed this sealing purposefully. She says she thinks she was always asking too much of you. She is generous that way, isn't she? She says you didn't mean to become 'so very alien' to her. I am not so sure. I love my wife. But I've never told her how I once knew a man in Beatty with a '66 Chevelle. I know what men like us are capable of.

Duane Moser, what I come back to is this: how could you have left M.'s letters by the side of Cane Springs Road near the ghost town Rhyolite where hardly anyone goes any more? (In fact, I have never seen another man out on Cane Springs Road. I drive out there to be alone. Maybe you do, too. Or you did, anyway.) Did you not realize that someone just like you might find them? How could you have left her again?

I have called the phone number listed on the prescription bottles, finally, though all I heard was the steady rising tones of the disconnected signal. Still, I found myself listening for you there. Please, write soon.

Truly,

Thomas Grey
PO Box 129, Verdi
Nevada 89439

PS On second thoughts, perhaps sometimes these things
are best left by the side of the road, as it were. Sometimes
a person wants a part of you that's no good. Sometimes
love is a wound that opens and closes, opens and closes, all
our lives.

> *November 2*
> Duane Moser
> 1077 Pincay Drive
> Henderson, Nevada 89015

Dear Mr Moser

My wife found your pictures, the ones of the Chevelle. The
one you maybe got from a junkyard or from a friend, or
maybe it's been in your family for years, rotting in a garage
somewhere because after what happened nobody wanted to
look at it. I kept the pictures tucked behind the visor in my
truck, bound with a rubber band. I don't know why I kept
them. I don't know why I've kept your letters from M., or
your medications. I don't know what I would do if I found
what I am looking for.

When I was in high school I worked the graveyard shift
at a gas station in Beatty. It's still there, on the corner of I-95
and Highway 374, near the hot springs. Maybe you've been
there. It's a Shell station now, but back then it was called
Hadley's Fuel. I worked there forty, fifty hours a week.
Bill Hadley was a friend of my father's. He was a crazy
sonofabitch, as my father would say, who kept a shotgun

r the counter and always accused me of stealing from
ll or sleeping on the job when I did neither. I liked the
graveyard shift, liked being up at night, away from Pop,
listening to the tremors of the big walk-in coolers, the hum
of the fluorescent lights outside.

Late that spring a swarm of grasshoppers moved through
Beatty on their way out to the alfalfa fields down south.
They were thick and fierce, roaring like a thunderstorm in
your head. The hoppers ate anything green. In two days
they stripped the leaves from all the cottonwoods and
willows in town, then they moved on to the juniper and pine,
the cheat grass and bitter salt cedar. A swarm of them ate
the wool right off of Abel Prince's live sheep. Things got so
bad that the trains out to the mines shut down for a week
because the guts of the bugs made the rails too slippery.

The grasshoppers were drawn to the fluorescent lights
at Hadley's. For weeks the parking lot pulsed with them. I
would have felt them crunch under my feet when I walked
out to the pumps that night, dead and dying under my
shoes, only I never made it out to the pumps. I was doing
schoolwork at the counter, calculus, for God's sake. I looked
up and the guy was already coming through the door at me.
I looked outside and saw the '66 Chevelle, gleaming under
the lights, grasshoppers falling all around it like rain.

I tried to stop him but he muscled back behind the
counter. He had a gun, held it like it was his own hand. He
said, You see this?

There was a bandanna over his face. But Beatty is a small
town and it was even smaller then. I knew who he was. I
knew his mother worked as a waitress at the Stagecoach and
that his sister had graduated the year before me. The money,
he was saying. His name was Frankie. The fucking money,
Frankie said.

I'd barely touched a gun before that night. I don't know

how I did it. I only felt my breath go out of me and reached under the counter to where the shotgun was and tried. I shot him in the head.

Afterwards, I called the cops. I did the right thing, they told me, the cops and Bill Hadley in his pyjamas, even my father. They said it over and over again. I sat on the kerb outside the store listening to them inside, their boots squeaking on the tile. The deputy sheriff, Dale Sullivan, who was also the assistant coach of the basketball team, came and sat beside me. I had my hands over my head to keep the grasshoppers away. Kid, it was bound to happen, Dale said. The boy was a troublemaker. A waste of skin.

He told me I could go on home. I didn't ask what would happen to the car.

That night, I drove out on Cane Springs Road to Rhyolite. I drove around that old ghost town with the windows rolled down, listening to the gravel pop under my tyres. The sun was coming up. There, in the milky light of dawn, I hated Beatty more than I ever had. The Stagecoach, the hot springs, all the trees looking so naked against the sky. I'd never wanted to see any of it ever again.

I was already on my way to college and everyone knew it. I didn't belong in Beatty. The boy's family, his mother and sister and stepfather, moved away soon after it happened. I'd never see them around town, or at Hadley's. For those last few weeks of school no one talked about it, at least not to me. Soon it was as though it had never happened. But – and I think I realized this then, up in Rhyolite, that dead town picked clean – Beatty would never be a place I could come home to.

When my wife asked about your pictures, she said she didn't realize I knew so much about cars. I said, Yeah, sure. Well, some. See the vents there? On the hood? See the blackout grille? That's how you know it's a '66. I told her I'd been thinking about buying an old car, fixing it up, maybe this one. Right then she just started laughing her head off. Sure, she managed through all her laughter, fix up a car. She kept on laughing. She tossed the bundle of photos on the seat of the truck and said, You're shitting me, Tommy.

It's not her fault. That man, the one who knows a '66 when he sees one, that's not the man she married. That's how it has to be. You understand, don't you?

I smiled at her. No, ma'am, I said. I wouldn't shit you. You're my favourite turd.

She laughed – she's generous that way – and said, A car. That's the last thing we need around here.

When I was a boy my father took me hunting. Quail mostly and, one time, elk. But I was no good at it and he gave up. I didn't have it in me, my father said, sad and plain as if it were a birth defect, the way I was. Even now, deer come down from the mountains and root in our garden, stripping our tomatoes from the vine, eating the hearts of our baby cabbages. My father says, Kill one. String it up. They'll learn. I tell him I can't do that. I spend my Sundays patching the holes in the fence, or putting up a taller one. The Church of the Compassionate Heart, my wife calls it. It makes her happy, this life of ours, the man I am. Layla helps me mend the fence. She stands behind me and hands me my pliers or my wire cutters when I let her.

But here's the truth, Duane Moser. Sometimes I see his eyes above that bandanna, see the grasshoppers leaping in the lights, hear them vibrating. I feel the kick of the rifle butt in my sternum. I would do it again.

Truly,
Thomas Grey
PO Box 129, Verdi
Nevada 89439

December 20
Duane Moser
1077 Pincay Drive
Henderson, Nevada 89015

Dear Duane Moser

This will be the last I write to you. I went back to Rhyolite. I told my wife I was headed south to camp and hike for a few days. She said, Why don't you take Layla with you? It would be good for her.

Layla slept nearly the whole drive. Six hours. When I slowed the car and pulled on to Cane Springs Road she sat up and said, Dad, where are we?

I said, We're here.

I helped her with her coat and mittens and we took a walk through the ruins. I told her what they once were. Here, I said, was the schoolhouse. They finished it in 1909. By then there weren't enough children in town to fill it. It burnt down the next year. She wanted to go closer.

I said, Stay where I can see you.

Why? she said.

I didn't know how to say it. Crumbling buildings, rotted-out floors, sinkholes, open mine shafts. Coyotes, rattlesnakes, mountain lions.

Because, I said. It's not safe for little girls.

We went on. There behind the fence is the post office, completed in 1908. This slab, these beams, that wall of brick, that was the train station. It used to have marble floors, mahogany woodworking, one of the first telephones in the state. But those have been sold or stolen over the years.

Why? she said.

That's what happens when a town dies.

Why?

Because, sweetheart. Because.

At dusk I tried to show Layla how to set a tent and build a fire but she wasn't interested. Instead she concentrated on filling her pink vinyl backpack with stones and using them to build little pyramids along the path that led out to the town. She squatted over them, gingerly turning the stones to find a flat side, a stable base. What are those for? I asked.

For if we get lost, she said. Pop Pop showed me.

When it got dark we sat together listening to the hiss of the hot dogs at the ends of our sticks, the violent sizzle of sap escaping the firewood. Layla fell asleep in my lap. I carried her to the tent and zipped her inside a sleeping bag. I stayed and watched her there, her chest rising and falling, hers the small uncertain breath of a bird.

When I bent to step out through the opening of the tent something fell from the pocket of my overalls. I held it up in the fire light. It was a cloudy stump of amethyst, as big as a horse's tooth.

I've tried, Duane Moser, but I can't picture you at 1077 Pincay Drive. I can't see you in Henderson period, out in the suburbs, on a cul-de-sac, in one of those prefab houses with the stucco and the garage gaping off the front like a mouth. I can't see you standing like a bug under those street lights the colour of antibacterial soap. At home at night I sit on my porch and watch the lights of Reno over the hills, the city marching out at us like an army. It's no accident that the first step in what they call developing a plot of land is to put a fence around it.

I can't see you behind a fence. When I see you, I see you here, at Rhyolite, harvesting sticks of charcoal from the half-burnt schoolhouse and writing your name on the exposed concrete foundation. Closing one eye to look through the walls of Jim Kelly's bottle house. No, that's my daughter. That's me as a boy getting charcoal stains on my blue jeans. That's you in your Chevelle, the '66, coming up Cane Springs Road, tearing past what was once the Porter Brothers' Store. I see you with M., flinging Fritos and meat and half-full cans of Coke and Bud Light from the car like a goddamn celebration, a shedding of your old selves.

It's almost Christmas. I've looked at the prescriptions, the letters, the photos. You're not Frankie, I know this. It's just a coincidence, a packet of pictures flung from a car out in the middle of nowhere. The car is just a car. The world is full of Chevelles, a whole year's worth of the '66. You know nothing of Hadley's fuel in Beatty, of a boy who was killed there one night in late spring when the grasshoppers were so loud they sounded like a thunderstorm in your head. I don't owe you anything.

When I woke this morning there was snow on the ground and Layla was gone. I pulled my boots on and walked around the camp. A layer of white covered the hills and the valley and the skeletons of the old buildings, lighting the valley fluorescent. It was blinding. I called my daughter's name. I listened, pressing the sole of my shoe against the blackened rocks lining the fire pit. I watched the snow go watery within my boot print. There was no answer.

I checked the truck. It was empty. In the tent I found her coat and mittens. Her shoes had been taken. I scrambled up a small hill and looked for her from there. I scanned for the shape of her among the old buildings, on the hills, along Cane Springs Road. Fence posts, black with moisture, strung across the valley like tombstones. Sickness thickened in my gut and my throat. She was gone.

I called for her again and again. I heard nothing, though surely my own voice echoed back to me. Surely the snow creaked under my feet when I walked through our camp and out to the ruins. Surely the frozen tendrils of creosote whipped against my legs when I began to run through the ghost town, up and down the gravel path. But all sound had left me except for a low, steady roaring, the sound of my own blood in my ears, of a car rumbling up the old road.

Suddenly my chest was burning. I couldn't breathe. Layla Layla. I crouched and pressed my bare palms against the frozen earth. The knees of my long johns soaked through, my fingers began to sting.

Then I saw a shape near the burnt remains of the schoolhouse. A panic as hot and fierce as anything – fiercer – rose in me. The slick pink vinyl of her backpack. I ran to it.

When I bent to pick it up I heard something on the wind. Something like the high, breathy language my daughters speak to each other when they play. I followed the sound around behind the schoolhouse and found Layla squatting there in her pyjamas, softly stacking one of her stone markers in the snow.

Hi, Dad, she said. The snow had reddened her hands and cheeks as though she'd been burnt. She handed me a stone. Here you go, she said.

I took my daughter by the shoulders and stood her up. I raised her sweet chin so her eyes met mine and then I slapped her across the face. She began to cry. I held her. The Chevelle drove up and down Cane Springs Road, the gravel under its tyres going pop pop pop. I said, Shh. That's enough. A child means nothing out here.

Truly,
Thomas Grey

THE MAGAZINE OF NEW WRITING

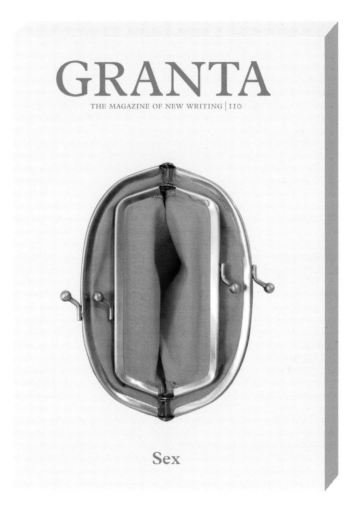

GRANTA.COM/UK111

Subscribe now,
or give *Granta* as a gift
and save up to £22 by taking out
a year-long subscription (4 issues):

UK
£34.95
(£29.95 Direct Debit)

Europe
£39.95

Rest of the world★
£45.95

Subscribe now at Granta.com/UK111
or by Freephone 0500 004 033
(quoting ref: UK111)

★Excluding USA, Canada and Latin America

GRANTA.COM/UK111

ONE HUNDRED
FEARS OF
SOLITUDE

THE GREATEST GENERATION GAP

Hal Crowther

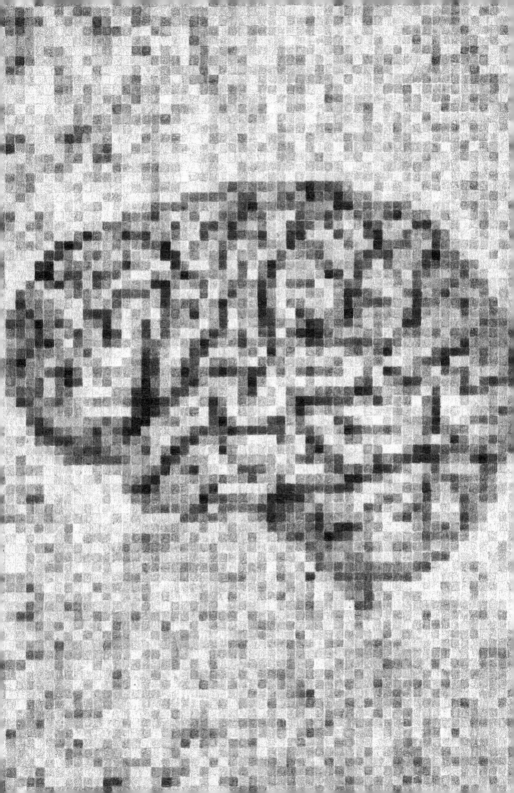

According to the terms of her will, Marguerite Yourcenar's house in Northeast Harbor, Maine, is preserved exactly as she left it when she died in 1987. The cottage she called Petite Plaisance is now in the devoted custody of her friend Yvon Bernier, a former professor of literature from Quebec, who lives in the house and conducts tours, by appointment, during those summer months when Maine swarms with visitors. The tourist traffic is never heavy at Petite Plaisance. The seriousness of Yourcenar's work has limited her celebrity; her shrine doesn't advertise itself and children under twelve are forbidden. Yvon Bernier, ever gracious, discourages the inquisitive day tripper by asking innocently, 'You are readers of her books, of course?' and pausing for you to offer him assurance or develop cold feet.

I think Bernier would prefer to give his talk in French, yet his English is fluent. He's proud and protective of this odd, almost miniaturized nineteenth-century cottage so crammed with books, art objects and curiosities that even a mildly boisterous eleven-year-old would create instant havoc. A tour of Petite Plaisance is, as she intended, like walking through the public rooms of Yourcenar's remarkable mind. 'This was a very quiet place,' said Bernier, explaining that there was no television, no radio, no electronic intrusion of any kind except for a vintage turntable where classical music might occasionally set a mood. The Belgian Yourcenar and her American companion, Grace Frick, were contemplative women of another century who kept a quiet house with a quiet garden, on a quiet street.

A few miles away, as the crow flies – but a couple of hours by station wagon, up and down these granite peninsulas – is Forest Farm, where the radical social critic and back-to-the-earth visionary Scott Nearing, author of *Living the Good Life*, lived the last third of his hundred-year life. Nearing and his wife Helen preached and practised integrity through subsistence farming, self-respect earned by eliminating every area of dependence on a capitalist system they detested. The Nearings were famous Luddites. Step Six of 'Our Design for Living' (they were also infamous list-makers) is 'holding down to the barest minimum the number of implements, tools, gadgets and machines which we might buy from the assembly lines of big business'. Into the late twentieth century they farmed almost entirely with hand tools, like Third World peasants, and refused even to convert their hand-cranked cement mixer to power.

Silence may have eluded the Nearings in the summertime, especially during the sixties when Earth-worshipping, Answer-seeking hippies came in droves to sit at their feet. But every summer sound was a human sound. In the dead of winter, in this remote cove off a dead-end road, among these homely stone buildings and walled gardens that overlook a frozen gravel beach, the silence must have been Arctic, interstellar, intergalactic.

Scott Nearing was born in 1883, Helen Nearing and Marguerite Yourcenar twenty years later. They were turn-of-the-century intellectuals who cheerfully confessed to looking back, rather than forward, for the keys to the lives they chose to lead. Yourcenar's most famous books illuminate the Middle Ages and the early Roman Empire. These were people whose ideals and predilections placed them far, far from the modern American mainstream. Yet they were here with us just yesterday – Scott and Yourcenar died while Ronald Reagan was president, Helen lived until 1995.

Not long after visiting these modest shrines to households where hard work and heavy thinking were done with medieval tools in medieval solitude, I read the back-to-school edition of the *New York Times* 'Circuits' section with my usual stunned incomprehension and a heightened sense of alarm. The electronic gadgets that have become standard equipment for a twenty-first-century undergraduate bear generic names, brand names, acronyms, model and serial numbers (DVP-CX995? PIXMA MP760??) that no doubt mean something to many, but nothing whatsoever to me. A *Times* reporter interviewed a Duke undergraduate named Eddy Leal, who confessed to owning a battery of three laptops with multifarious accessories ('It's like another world in my dorm room') as well as, of course, a cellphone and a 500-song iPod which are, he says, 'with me no matter where I am – I wouldn't mind if I could have them implanted in my body'.

'I know, it's kind of crazy,' said Leal of his three-computer installation, guessing that he was eccentrically overwired – but guessing wrong. Other students in this same article boasted even more bewildering batteries of personal hardware, far beyond my vocabulary to describe. Returning college students in the USA now spend more than $8 billion to rewire themselves, two-thirds of what they'll spend on textbooks, and of course each year the gap decreases.

The long-term implications of mechanized education are overwhelming, but first let's deal with the subject of silence. I'm not ancient, yet my college education forty-plus years ago was pre-technological, by current lights antediluvian. Though telephones and television had been invented, none of us, not even the most affluent, had installed them in our rooms, far less on our bodies. My fraternity house contained one of each, a battered basement TV set with a small clientele and a payphone next to which we waited for hours, playing cards and drinking beer and coffee, for our turns to call home or plead our cases with identically isolated Holyoke girls. Cellphones and email had not yet made their appearance in science fiction. Ninety-eight per cent of communication was verbal and face-to-face. If you had an urgent message for someone, you stuffed a note in his box at the student union or trudged half a mile across an ice-bound campus and hoped you'd find him in. Only juniors and seniors were allowed to drive cars.

Winter or summer, that was a lonely walk, silent, a time to think without threat of interruption. Blessedly disconnected. 'Alone with his thoughts', now a literary anachronism, was a commonplace reality. Without that freedom to disconnect, then and now, I for one would have gone raving mad. And at this point most readers under forty-five may disconnect and consign me to some historical novel by Marguerite Yourcenar. How could Eddy Leal understand that if a cellphone and an iPod were implanted in my body, I'd pay virtually any price to have them removed?

Computers and allied technologies have created the most intimidating generation gap in human history, one so wide and so rapidly created that I stand staring across the chasm like an aborigine watching Krakatoa split the sky. In age we're much nearer to our children than to Yourcenar or the Nearings, but technologically – and in a new sense psychologically – we're nearer to Louis XIV. Our college experience bore no resemblance to the one available at Duke University in 2008; it was more like the one Roger Bacon would have found at Oxford in 1260. The difference, the distance is incalculable.

The value of silence, of solitude, has never before been disputed. Fifty years ago Patrick Leigh Fermor, another wise seeker of my parents' generation, wrote an account of his experiences as a guest at several famous French monasteries, including La Grande Trappe, where the Trappist rule of absolute silence is observed. *A Time to Keep Silence* is a book of such manifest insight and sympathy that pre-wired Westerners took it much to heart, and many of its readers were tempted to sample the monastic life themselves. Leigh Fermor, in his nineties, is still with us. If he's kept abreast of the technological tsunami, he must wonder what the cellphone and email armies would make of his book. Even then, in that first decade of Queen Elizabeth II's reign, modern urban life was complex and often conducted at nerve-shattering decibels. Leigh Fermor wrote of 'automatic drains, such as conversation at meals, small talk, catching trains, or the hundred anxious trivialities that poison everyday life' – anxieties, he claims, which vanished from memory after a few weeks with the monks, leaving him 'nineteen hours a day of absolute and god-like freedom'. Re-entry was excruciating. A few hours back to Paris on the train, and the world outside the abbey's walls struck him as 'an inferno of noise and vulgarity entirely populated by bounders and sluts and crooks'.

To me, that sounds like a prophetic glimpse of the world we inhabit today. There may be very few ways in which the Dark Ages – Leigh Fermor visited the Abbey of St Wandrille, founded in AD 649 – compare favourably to the twenty-first century. Yet here he finds an important one. Mere small talk, that time-wasting 'anxious triviality' he escaped in the cloister, has become the sacrament, equivalent to the monks' constant prayer, by which hyper-technology's initiates declare and share their faith. A Stanford undergraduate, Sam Altman, once walked out of a huge lecture hall and observed that, 'Two hundred students all pulled out their cellphones, called someone, and said, "Where are you?" People want to connect.' Altman's response was to found a company called Loopt, which with the aid of GPS chips in cellphones enables cellmates to track each other, literally, twenty-four hours a day. 'PRIVACY LOST: THESE PHONES CAN FIND YOU' was the sceptical headline. But Daniel Graf, founder of a similar networking service, was excited to announce, 'Now you can share your life over a mobile phone, and someone is always connected, watching.'

Not long ago, it was generally accepted that humanity's most creative achievements, from art and poetry to major scientific discoveries, were the precious fruits of solitude. But in a single heartbeat on history's timeline, this sacred, fecund privacy has become the unpardonable social sin for the generation on which future creativity depends. In her introduction to *A Time to Keep Silence*, Karen Armstrong, a former nun and historian of religion, writes, 'Our world is even more noisy than it was in the 1950s, when Leigh Fermor wrote this book: piped music and mobile phones jangle ceaselessly, and silence and solitude are shunned as alien and unnatural.'

'You've got a generation that doesn't have the same concept of privacy and personal boundaries as generations before,' understates child psychologist David Verhaagen. I've tried to explain to young people that unspoiled privacy is the most important thing a person like me could ever ask from his life. Pissing it away for a fistful of electronic candy seems incomprehensibly pathetic. Just so they know where I stand. Urgent warnings that technology is recklessly exposing our darkest secrets to every eager peeping Tom – official, corporate or criminal – fall on deaf (or at least numb and overtaxed) ears. The traditional concept of privacy, which anchors our Bill of Rights, is a tough sell to technophiliacs who spend half their waking hours on sites like MySpace and YouTube, recklessly exposing themselves. The most recent Kaiser Family Foundation study (in January 2010) factored in multitasking and found that eight- to eighteen-year-olds log an average daily exposure of just under eleven hours of electronic media. An increase of two hours daily since 2004, it includes computers and social networks, cellphones, instant messaging, TV, video games and iPods. Media consume nearly all their waking hours when they're not in school.

Privacy has deep, deep roots in Western civilization, yet a few mediocre gadgets uprooted it in less than a decade. Who knew the young were so lonely, so susceptible, so desperate for connection? Who's to blame for their loneliness, for their seduction and metamorphosis into electro-cyborgs who bear only a physical resemblance to their parents? What sort of lives were they leading before they were wired? It's as if prisoners buried in the dungeons of the Château d'If, with no previous communication except tapping on the stone walls of their separate cells, were suddenly issued mobile phones with email. What else but a compulsive frenzy of messaging, no content required? Indulging America's children with all the best that money could buy, did we somehow build cruel prisons instead of stately mansions for their souls?

Whatever we offered them was the wrong thing, or not enough. When the Pied Piper came they marched away behind him, hooked forever on his first plaintive note. Who was the Piper, if we had to give him a face? Bill Gates, Steven Jobs? Digital products seemed harmless enough in the beginning, meeting obvious demands for faster, more efficient commercial communication. Business will have its way. But the personal computer and all its derivative technology were not so obvious, not to most of us now left behind. We were sure it was boring – to liberal arts majors of my vintage, most tools more complex than a hammer are invisible. We never dreamed it was more addictive than heroin. 'I lost my cellphone once,' a twenty-five-year-old woman with a master's degree told a reporter. 'I felt like my world had just ended. I had a breakdown on campus.'

Perhaps the child of a wired woman is weaned from silence in the womb. Has the genetic code itself been altered, in ten years' time, by personal technology? Bill Gates may be remembered as one of the most significant philanthropists of all time; if his grand crusade against tobacco is successful, no doubt he'll save millions of lives. But his legacy as the godfather of computer language will affect many more human lives, perhaps in ways painful to contemplate. Gates the philanthropist is well aware that history will judge him on both scores. The Piper is a troubling figure, and all his wealth can't buy back the children we have lost.

Computer scientist and artist Jaron Lanier, a Silicon Valley heavyweight who was a pioneer in the development of virtual reality, decries online culture as 'a culture of reaction without action', at its nastiest 'a culture of sadism'. In his book, *You Are Not A Gadget*, the disillusioned Lanier portrays the cybersphere as a 'hive mind' buzzing with little but trivia, acrimony and 'a persistent somnolence'. His conclusion? 'We will only escape it when we kill the hive.'

Some of the wizards who fathered the digital revolution have had similar misgivings. The late Joseph Weizenbaum, an MIT mathematician and computer scientist who authored one of the first conversational computer programs, became a profound sceptic about technology's influence on the human condition. Weizenbaum, who was a child in Nazi Germany, believed that obsessive reliance on technology was a moral failure in society and an invitation to fascism.

His book, *Computer Power and Human Reason*, a humanist argument for vigilance against technological dependency, was published in 1976. Weizenbaum's scepticism was shared by American computer pioneer and mogul Max Palevsky, who died recently at eighty-five. Palevsky, founder of the computer-chip giant Intel, told an interviewer in 2008, 'I don't own a computer. I don't own a cellphone, I don't own any electronics. I do own a radio.'

Given decades to reflect on what they wrought, it's eerie that many of the scientists who created our electronic cocoon sound like the scientists who worked on the atom bomb at Los Alamos. But Lanier's reflections on the 'hive mind' owe much to Sven Birkerts, who in 1994 published an eloquent, important book, *The Gutenberg Elegies*, which warned us against 'the prospect of a collective life in an electronic hive'. I revere Birkerts' book and recommend it, yet subsequent developments have rendered his dramatic conclusion quaint, quixotic, almost meaningless. 'Refuse it,' he says of the cyber-life, words that echo curiously when it is no longer possible to follow his advice.

The tide of tech will not be turned; the Piper won't bring back the lost boys and girls. Choose your most dog-eared metaphor: the levees have been breached, the train has left the station, the barn door stands open and your horse has fled. The wailing of the wire-wary only aggravates the captive multitudes and widens the dreadful gap. But we can't just fold our tents and quit the field because we, the pre-wired generations, bear most of the blame. We betrayed them. We turned them over to habit-forming, mind-altering, behaviour-warping gizmos when they were helpless children. There was almost no resistance. The Piper played and everybody danced. Politicians, colleges, school boards, doomed publishers and libraries and doomed media all welcomed these technologies uncritically, enthusiastically, like Stone Age savages fainting with wonder over a transistor radio. Americans have always been suckers for technology – our love affairs with automobiles, television and nuclear power haven't turned out well either. But this was the most pitiful submission, and may prove the most fateful.

Big business bet its whole ranch on the digital revolution and put everything in its awesome arsenal behind it. Nothing was left to chance, and there was no one strong enough to resist. Though I'm a man easily defeated and discouraged by machines – I've called myself an 'iron Luddite' and written a tearful farewell to my typewriter – I don't claim to be a purist or a hero of the resistance, such as it was. I bought a primitive Compaq laptop in 1993 because my computer phobia was creating extra work for my colleagues; after fourteen years impersonating a typewriter it died and I replaced it with a Dell. I finally opened an email account last January because people were emailing me anyway and the burden of it fell on my wife. At the same time I acquired a cellphone, also at my wife's insistence, though no one else knows the number. I have one shy foot set reluctantly in the way-wired twenty-first century; to Scott Nearing, if he'd lived to see this, I'm a craven sell-out.

My bad attitude persists because I've felt the chill force of coercion. Tell me I must and I'll tell you I won't; I've been that way since childhood. I've lost friends my own age – it isn't only the young – because they've invented a new language they insist on speaking, and I refuse to learn it. A devoted techie with no perspective is as lost to me as a friend who is born again. Some find my stubborn obsolescence amusing, others aggravating – even threatening. Coercion is not just interpersonal but societal, and pervasive. The word 'Luddite', which we used to wear with defiant pride, has become an epithet like 'communist' or 'reactionary'. Sven Birkerts' metaphor of the beehive cuts deep in several directions. The buzz inside and outside your head has murdered silence and reflection. But just as frightening is the harsh warning, explicit or implicit, that if you won't be wired into the hive you won't get your share of the honey. 'We'd better get it,' Birkerts wrote, 'lest we find ourselves stranded by the wayside, on some windy platform watching the express rattle by.'

We can't stop the big train. But it's our responsibility, imposed by our guilt, to flash yellow lights and hang signs on the station platform, warning of perils on the tracks ahead. No one denies the impact of these devices, or their usefulness. Who at my age, watching precious time fly, wouldn't bless email for the pointless time-consuming conversations it replaces? Who denies that Barack Obama's epic rout of the Republicans would have been impossible without his mastery of Internet communication? But with truly revolutionary technology no one stops to factor in the human cost. Though young people wired almost from birth have a hard time imagining a different life, an observer from outside the hive is unlikely to envy their lot. Chronic, epidemic obesity among American children, along with unprecedented levels of juvenile diabetes and heart disease, coincides exactly with the advent of 'personal technology'. An alarming study that followed 4,000 subjects for three decades indicates that 90 per cent of American men and 70 per cent of American women will eventually be fat. The only hope for the swollen, pasty-faced, short-of-breath victims of the electro-lifestyle may be an experimental drug, AICAR, that appears to have the same effect as exercise on laboratory mice. A brave new world where pills replace push-ups.

Worse news is that the American mind is emulating its body – it's turning to suet. A few years ago the educational benefits of the new technology were hyped hysterically, with futurists and investors predicting an intellectual renaissance anchored by computers. The reality seems to be just the opposite. Though the educational potential of the Internet is limitless, it's becoming apparent that wired students use technology less to learn than to distract themselves from learning, and to take advantage of toxic short cuts like research-paper databases and essay-writing websites. Teachers report that electronic cheating is pandemic.

The results are grimly predictable. Entrance exams administered by ACT Inc. establish that half the students now entering college in the USA lack the basic reading-comprehension skills to succeed in literature, history or sociology courses. Reading and writing skills among eighth-graders decline each year, as Internet penetration rises. Only 3 per cent now read at the level scored 'advanced', and the state of Maine recently scrapped its eighth-grade writing test because 78 per cent of the participants failed. Half the teenagers tested by the advocacy group Common Core could not place the Civil War in the second half of the nineteenth century, a quarter drew a blank on Adolf Hitler, a fifth failed to identify America's enemies in World War II. A third of America's high-school students drop out – one every twenty-six seconds – and two-thirds prove incapable of higher education. Though foreign students are known to embrace the cyber-life with equal enthusiasm, the demoralizing educational gap between the USA and developed nations of Europe and Asia grows wider every year.

Bill Gates, the Piper himself, has said, 'When I compare our high schools with what I see when I travel abroad, I am terrified for our workforce of tomorrow.'

Doubts are spreading, though perhaps too late. In the spring of 2007, Liverpool High School in upstate New York made national news when it abandoned its laptop programme as a failed experiment, and went back to books. 'After seven years there was literally no evidence it had any impact on student achievement – none,' said Mark Lawson, president of the Liverpool school board. While their test scores stagnated, Liverpool students used their laptops to cheat on exams, message friends, hack into local businesses, update Facebook profiles and download pornography. 'The teachers were telling us that when there's a one-to-one relationship between the student and the laptop, the machine gets in the way,' Lawson concluded. 'It's a distraction to the educational process.'

The teachers' rebellion against laptops has been reinforced by college professors, who find their wired students just as prone to inattention, Web surfing and promiscuous messaging. And dumber all the time. Anecdotal evidence is excruciating; Michael Skube, a professor of journalism and Pulitzer-winning former book critic, claims that he asked a class of seventeen college sophomores to name their favourite writers and extracted just one name – Dan Brown of *The Da Vinci Code* fame – from the lot of them. Technological saturation coincides precisely with a general decline in literacy. The National Assessment of Adult Literacy, a test administered just once a decade by the US Department of Education, found that between 1992 and 2003 the percentage of college graduates scoring 'proficient' or above in reading comprehension had shrunk from forty to thirty-one. America had lost roughly one quarter of its most sophisticated readers. No doubt most of them had died.

If not a third of our baccalaureates can now read 'lengthy complex English texts and draw complicated inferences', democracy itself is an empty exercise, an exercise in condescension. Little wonder that the high end of the publishing industry is on life support, that struggling newspapers jettison their book critics, that pedlars of the crudest, most cretinous right-wing propaganda publish non-fiction's most reliable best-sellers.

If intellectual stagnation and physical decay don't frighten you, consider evidence of severe psychological displacement, to the edge of madness and well beyond. Gordon Bell, a computer programmer, is a 'life-logger' who wears an audio recorder and a tiny camera set to take a picture every sixty seconds, so that everything Gordon sees, hears, says, reads or thinks for the rest of his life – he's seventy-three – is recorded for us to examine, if we should so choose. My primitive filing system can't keep up with the pathology reports. *New York Times*: 'A professionally dressed woman dove headfirst into an airport restaurant's garbage searching for her lost BlackBerry through half-eaten sandwiches and Kung Pao chicken.' *USA Today*: 'A rush to buy four-year-old used laptops turned into a violent stampede Tuesday at Richmond International Raceway. An estimated 5,500 people were vying for one of the 1,000 Apple iBooks that Henrico County schools were selling. Jesse Sandler, twenty, said he used a folding chair to beat back people who tried to cut in front of him. Seventeen people suffered minor injuries, with four requiring hospitalization.' *Associated Press*: 'Early Friday police responded to a call from a man who said his girlfriend was having trouble breathing. Officers arrived to find the woman with a cellphone lodged in her throat. Police were told that the boyfriend wanted the phone and the woman tried to swallow it.'

The Times also profiled William Donelson, a twenty-one-year-old computer science student 'so enthralled with the link between technology and the body that he has tattoos of data-input jacks running down his spine'. This pioneer had just had a body-piercing specialist implant a microchip between his thumb and forefinger, a radio-frequency identification device that enables him to log on to his computer, open doors, unlock his car and start appliances with a wave of his hand. Donelson, who also wears a wireless cellphone earpiece shaped like an earring, has become an actual cyborg, a walking amalgam of biology and technology. In the blink of an eye, what was science fiction or satire has become reportage. For all we know, Donelson was the model for the character Way Wired Willie in my favourite newspaper comic strip, Berke Breathed's recently expired *Opus*. WWW, who wears a huge headdress fashioned of coaxial cables, antennae and blinking electronic components, didn't show up much towards the end of the strip's run, which was all too brief. Was Willie a joke too many readers took personally?

Naturally psychiatry is taking full notice of techno-pathology. There's a Center for Internet Addiction Recovery in Bradford, Pennsylvania, and America's first residential treatment centre, reSTART, was established in 2009 in Fall City, Washington. reSTART offers a forty-five-day detox and rehab for patients addicted to Internet surfing, video games, texting, Facebook, eBay, Twitter and the like. (There are, incidentally, many such centres in China, South Korea and Taiwan, where cyber-dependency is epidemic.) Treatment of cyber-junkies is becoming a sub-specialty for cutting-edge psychiatrists like John Ratey of Harvard, who coined the term 'acquired attention deficit disorder' to describe their pathology, and Edward Hallowell, who invented the term 'screen sucking' for compulsive abuse of the BlackBerry, or 'CrackBerry', that has enslaved so many of his patients.

'A female patient asked me if I thought it was abnormal that her husband lays the BlackBerry on the bed when they make love,' Dr Hallowell related. 'I thought the fact that she even asked me was more extreme than what he did.'

And so it goes. I don't claim that hard-wired Americans are all fat, ignorant and crazy – only that they're at higher risk for all three than generations that preceded them. It's not a difficult case to make, not even for someone from a generation like mine, which chose to fry millions of healthy neurons with LSD, psilocybin, cannabis and cocaine. The walking wounded from that excess are still around, but most of us kicked our habits and descended safely from those treacherous highs. High tech is a habit too new to boast any record of survivors, recovering addicts, successful rehabs. So far, no one's coming back. In the words of recovery programmes, users have yet to acknowledge that they have a problem. Or that there is a problem. Staring for hours at glowing squares, gossiping with needy strangers, poking away at little pissant keyboards, playing half-assed violent games – does this strike anyone as an interesting and honourable life, or even a preparation for one? And the answer, more often than not, would come back, 'Sure, what's your problem?'

With that last outburst, I probably sacrifice half the readers I have left. But if you're offended or threatened, console yourself with the impotence and rapid extinction of my kind. We pose no threat to your habit. Technology's sceptics are ageing and thinning out. Soon, by conversion or attrition, they will vanish. Soon, when everyone is born wired into the hive, no more of them will appear.

All the more reason to have our say, leave our protests on the record, exit cursing and fighting. The health of the human animal – intellectual development, mental stability, cardiovascular fitness – will be the major issue in a wired world. Before long its decline may be too obvious to debate. We already miss the children we sold into electronic slavery. But there's so much more to dislike about our cocoon woven of wires, our house built of chips. Thieves, grifters and predators of every description have flourished in the cyber-forest; the signature crime of the twenty-first century is identity theft. The Internet is the greatest gift to the paedophile community since the Vatican stood its ground on celibate priests. But if you think these are all quibbles compared with the joy and comfort your hardware provides, try out your polished indifference on the prospect of environmental apocalypse.

'E-waste', as it's now called, is the sobering dark side to even the rosiest view of an all-wired future. In America in 2005, more than 1.5 million tons of discarded electronic devices ended up in landfills, where high tech's toxic metals, including lead, mercury, cadmium and beryllium, find their way into the soil, the water tables and the air. In China, which produces a million tons of e-waste annually and imports, for profit, 70 per cent of the world's lethal garbage (estimated at as much as 50 million tons), whistle-blowers are already blaming high rates of birth defects, infant mortality and blood diseases on e-waste. With their reliance on instant obsolescence and limited commitment to recycling, hardware manufacturers create an unmanageable flow of poisonous trash that the planet can't possibly tolerate: Americans alone discard 100 million computers, cellphones and related devices every year, at a rate of 136,000 per day. Half a billion of America's old cellphones sit in drawers, dead but not buried. There is no place and no plan for all this stuff. Our world has been wired by wildly inefficient technology – it takes roughly 1.8 tons of raw materials (fossil fuels, water, metal ores) to manufacture one PC and its monitor, and mining the gold needed for the circuit board of a single cellphone generates 220 pounds of waste.

These industries are self-evidently unsustainable. They are not environmentally sane. What happens when addicted masses can no longer get their e-fix? Your problem, not mine. What's left of me will be down there in that contaminated landfill with what's left of your iPhones. But the problem with an environmental alarm, no matter how imminent or concrete the peril, is that it hangs suspended in abstraction, a vision of the future that's hard to download as you sit there poking at your BlackBerry. Even colour photos of Ghanaian children scrounging through Accra's burning e-waste dumps for precious metals (courtesy of the *National Geographic*) don't cling to the everyday conscience, unless perhaps you convert one of them into a screen saver. The cyclopean gap between old and new, the rapid, almost overnight change in the human equation is the more urgently compelling theme, even for an environmental alarmist like me.

You on the far side of the great digital divide, you're not like us. But that's the lament of every washed-up generation, and irrelevant. What bothers me isn't that you're not like us, but that you're too much like each other. The unwired remnant, a dwindling minority, is smugly dismissed as the pitifully old, the desperately poor, a few reactionary eccentrics and a bozo brigade so technologically challenged that they wound themselves with electric razors. Not so. The unconverted aren't predictably left or right, either. What we have in common, besides grey hair and a long previous life undisturbed by the murmur of microchips, is a commitment to autonomy – a conviction, widespread in our long-ago prime, that the best part of each of us is the part that never swims in the mainstream. We also believe that the mainstream is shallower, more polluted and clogged with swimmers than it was in our day.

What else? We share a guilty certainty that the race of innocents we consigned to the beehive is living a life of closed circuits – a no-exit Guantánamo of the spirit. At some finite point, multiplying human connections no longer expands our consciousness, but begins to suffocate it. Sven Birkerts referred to what is lost in the beehive as 'soul'. 'My use of soul is secular,' he wrote. 'Soul is our inwardness, our self-reflectiveness, our orientation to the unknown. Soul waxes in private, wanes in public . . . Soul is private. Solitary.'

Huddling together and sharing everything is not exactly the American tradition, the American way – it's the opposite of the individualist mythology that gave us Daniel Boone, Honest Abe and Billy the Kid. It doesn't fit either with young America's hunger to be rich, a goal shared by 80 per cent of Americans aged eighteen to twenty-five. In our society riches come to innovators and ruthless, visionary entrepreneurs – never to reliable company men who wait their turn. Fame, a goal of 51 per cent of these same young people, nearly always eludes the conformist. Where is the pantheon devoted to famous members of mobs, herds, hives, bureaucracies? Only the outsider, the dissenter, the rule-breaker ever made his weight felt in a time of significant change.

Peer pressure and the herd instinct are the things about human beings that suck most of all – to use a strong pejorative familiar to the wired generation. They're what made Mark Twain curl his lip when he referred to 'man's commonest weakness, his aversion to being unpleasantly conspicuous, pointed at, shunned, as being on the unpopular side . . . Its other name is Moral Cowardice, and is the commanding feature of the make-up of 9,999 men in the 10,000.' Twain liked to exaggerate, but a hundred years ago he saw the exhaustion of the independent spirit that made America possible (his essay was 'The United States of Lyncherdom'), and the threat to freedom when everyone knows, and cares, what everyone else is thinking. The only thing Twain couldn't imagine was the technology to turn a million timid brains into one giant brain, still timid.

Technophiles hail the breakthroughs in online fund-raising and instant, high-tech communication that cleared a path to victory for the first black president – the first BlackBerry president too, which in the long run may prove just as historic. Bloggers appear to believe in virtual revolution, in coups executed at the keyboard instead of in the streets. But I think they miss the deeper political implications of the big-hive model. In spite of the election, the USA I see is gullible, incurious, passive and preoccupied. For political and commercial purposes we're easy to manipulate, but there are so many of us that we used to be hard to keep track of. The answer was personal technology, a corporate Trojan Horse that America welcomed with fireworks and marching bands, and the support of an overwhelming majority of politicians and educators. The likely result will be the wet dream of every overt and closet totalitarian – a submissive population of consumers and employees, tightly wired and monitored and purged of rogue individuals. Your friends will have you triangulated and so will your boss, your government and every hungry salesman who cares. Privacy, under siege as never before, is the key to it all. The fewer people who know what you're thinking or even where you are or what you're doing, the more dangerous you become to people who hope to control you.

'We live in an age when private life is being destroyed,' Milan Kundera said in 1985. 'The police destroy it in communist countries, journalists threaten it in democratic countries, and little by little the people themselves lose their taste for private life and their sense of it. Without secrecy, nothing is possible – not love, not friendship.'

Some of technology's most furious political and sociological critics focus on the expansion of the work week and the virtual workplace – now everywhere and inescapable, fastened to your belt or pinned to your ear. A decade before they were fully wired, Americans passed the Japanese to become the most overworked workforce in the developed world. Now devices like the BlackBerry chain even managers and high-salaried professionals to a twenty-four-hour clock that figures to burn them out more rapidly than nineteenth-century wage slaves. Wired America doesn't rest, and who benefits from that? Long before the computer was a twinkle in Thomas Watson's eye, John E. Edgerton, president of the National Association of Manufacturers, said something (circa 1925) that enemies of the wired workplace love to note and quote: 'The emphasis should be put on work – more work and better work. Nothing breeds radicalism more than leisure.'

Of all the artists and thinkers who've rejected the cyber-revolution, perhaps the most emphatic was the late American poet, publisher, and photographer Jonathan Williams, who divided his distinctly original life between the North Carolina mountains and the Yorkshire Dales. 'I have a feeling about the Internet,' Williams wrote. 'I think it's the younger sister of the Gorgon Medusa. If you look more than about twice you're going to get turned into stone or something much worse, more unpleasant.'

For the last word, it seems appropriate to return to those solemn voices from the recent past, from the Maine silence where this meditation began. Marguerite Yourcenar offers her prophecy in the words of the Roman emperor Hadrian (AD 76–138): 'I doubt if all the philosophy in the world can succeed in suppressing slavery; it will, at most, change the name. I can well imagine forms of servitude worse than our own, because more insidious, whether they transform men into stupid, complacent machines, who believe themselves free just when they are most subjugated, or whether to the exclusion of leisure and pleasures essential to man they develop a passion for work as violent as the passion for war among barbarous races. To such bondage for the human mind and imagination I prefer even our avowed slavery.' (*Memoirs of Hadrian*, 1951)

And this is Scott Nearing, from his book *Living the Good Life*, published in 1970: 'Machine tools are a novelty, recently introduced into the realm of human experience. There can be no question but that machines have more power than humans. Also there can be no question but that they have watered down or annihilated many of the most ancient, most fascinating and creative human skills, broken up established institutions, pushed masses of "hands" into factories and herded droves of anonymous footloose wanderers from urban slum to urban slum. Only the historian of the future will be able to assess the net effect of the machine age on human character and on man's joy in being and his will to live.' ■

The Door Was Open and the House Was Dark

IN MEMORY OF DAVID HAMMOND

The door was open and the house was dark
Wherefore I called his name, although I knew
The answer this time would be silence

That kept me standing listening while it grew
Backwards and down and out into the street
Where as I'd entered (I remember now)

The streetlamps too were out.
I felt, for the first time there and then, a stranger,
Intruder almost, wanting to take flight

Yet well aware that here there was no danger,
Only withdrawal, a not unwelcoming
Emptiness, as in a midnight hangar

On an overgrown airfield in high summer.

GRANTA

LETTERS

Iris Murdoch

Between 1946 and 1975, Iris Murdoch corresponded with the
French poet and novelist Raymond Queneau, a successful author
sixteen years her senior. Published for the first time, the letters here
are part of a collection recently acquired by the Centre for
Iris Murdoch Studies at Kingston University, London.

It is likely that Murdoch destroyed all of Queneau's letters to her.

I know you are very busy
but may I nevertheless
point out that I haven't
had a letter from you since
(I think) July. I know too
that I didn't write for a
long time, but I am hoping
that you are not cross with
me. Vous ne m'en voulez pas?

Well now (your letter of 10 July) – I am truly <u>very</u> sorry to have been, even for a moment, a further problem & embarrassment for you. Thank you however for writing frankly. Please don't think that I 'expect' anything of you – beyond, I hope, your continued friendship. We have expressed to each other our sincere 'sympathie' – that remains, I think? For the rest, our ways lie pretty far apart and I see no reason why our relationship should be a problem for either. Please, please don't distress yourself about it. I well realize that your moral and emotional situation must be most unhappy – I sympathise very profoundly. I <u>will</u> <u>not</u> <u>be</u> a complicating factor. You know that I care about all this; I <u>have</u> become very attached to you & shall certainly remain so, but I don't think there is any cause for agitation in that.

I am trying to work, but London is more nerve rending than ever. I have finished 'Etre et le Néant', thank God, with much admiration & some flutters of criticism. It stops just where I want to begin; I suppose I shall now have to do some thinking for myself. (Or shall I just wait till Sartre publishes his *Ethics*?) MacKinnon at Oxford seems to be going through some sort of spiritual crisis & can't see me. A bunch of goddamn neurotics I have for friends. I have continued a little with *Pierrot* & find this the one soothing occupation in a somewhat ragged world.

Thank you very much for 'Les Ziaux', which I have not yet had time to read. Work well at Avignon & don't worry yourself to death. I wish you most heartily the strength to solve your problems.

Now & always I remain your calm tender devoted reader & friend.

Iris

PS My surname ends with an H not a K. Pax tecum –

24 April 1947
4 Eastbourne Road
Chiswick
London W4

[. . .]

I was most glad to have your news, or rather lack of news, abstention from news. How bloody of Dial Press to have second thoughts now – still, I imagine it means only delay? I hope Lehmann hurries up with his project for our island. I feel most impatient to see you in English. I hope your play is going down well? But most of all I long for *Gueule de Pierre III*. (If the devil were bargaining with me for my soul, I think what could tempt me most would be the ability to write as well as you. Tho' when I reflect, in my past encounters with that character he has not lacked other good bargaining points –)

For the rest – I am glad that you have reasons for being happier, even if you don't yet fully profit by them. Confidences – yes, I know, I too would like to 'talk' – but perhaps I'd better not, for the moment anyway. Also there are some things which it is almost impossible to explain, to expose, however violently one wishes to. (Another language problem.) Spoken of they seem . . . melodrama, or an attempt to trip the other into complicity. Yet for all that I'd like to talk with you frankly one day (about my own histories, I mean). You are important to me in all sorts of ways. As a symbol, yes – one distant undiscovered magnetic pole of my own uncertain mind. But as yourself too – a voice in my life, and more, yourself, with your curious laugh and nervous ways. Perhaps I behaved foolishly in Paris (forgive me) but my affection for you was then and is now most most sincere and tender.

After much indecision about jobs, I've decided to apply for two next month – one a year-long studentship at Cambridge, & the other a lecturership in philosophy at Liverpool university. I don't know what my chances are for either. The Cambridge thing is to be applied for by June 1st – rather late in the year, so that hanging on for that means letting go various jobs which I might chase after now. But I yearn for Cambridge. (Oxford is intolerable to me now – I can't help tho' wanting to 'start again' in another city which is exactly like Oxford but all different.) – This thing is competitive however, & I daresay I shan't get it. So – Liverpool, or else Bradford Technical Institute – or God knows what yet more frightful hack task in some red brick town in some marsh in the midlands. *On verra.*

[. . .]I'd like to talk with you – this afternoon, say – enormously at leisure, sitting outside some café in the Boulevard something-or-other, with the sparrows hopping on the table, & the people passing. And discuss Universal History and Human Destiny and our history & our destiny, and politics and language – I need so much to talk & talk – but the chances so rarely come.

I hope that, truly, life goes better with you. I wish you very well. Pardon me if I say things amiss. I am deeply concerned that you should be happy & solve your problems. Write if you've time, but never mind if you haven't. More news from me later. Fiat pax in virtute tua.

Devotedly, your
I

21 Sep 1947
4 Eastbourne Road
Chiswick, W4

My dear, I am back in London, God help me. There is the usual collection of nerve rending letters waiting, inter alia, a ms of mine (a novel written in '44) politely rejected by a publisher – & a request from a learned body that I should lecture on existentialism in London in the autumn. [. . .] I feel alarm at this – sometimes I think my playing the philosopher is a great hoax & one day someone will denounce me. You see already I'm fretting about these trifles. But not all trifles – some distressing letters too from sad friends.

You said that love between a man & a woman made always some sort of basis for life. Yes. Yet how rarely it occurs without hurt to one or both parties – or rather both, for if one is hurt both are hurt. Yet I don't know – I can't tell for other people really, only for myself.

I meant all I said last night – but don't be distressed – very simply & loyally. I hope & pray we won't ever harm each other. I'm very tired at the moment – sort of drunk with tiredness & nothing to eat, you know the way one can be. My parents are out playing cards. It's late. I can't help wishing for simple things, simple solutions. I wish I could see you often & get to know you. Maybe I will get to know you better in time.

I'll write again in a few days when I'm feeling less feverish. Thank you, for very many things. I'm happy that I know you and happy that I love you.
I'm so glad you like Prince Myshkin.
I hope all goes very well with all your projects.
Most tenderly

I am yours
I

24 August 1952

I'm sorry about the scene on the bridge – or rather, I'm sorry in the sense that I ought either to have said nothing or to have said something sooner. I was in extreme pain when I came to see you chez Gallimard on Friday – but what with English habitual reticence, and your cool way of keeping me at a distance I could say nothing altho' I wanted desperately to take you in my arms.

On the other hand, if I had started to talk sooner I might have spent the rest of the time (such as it was) in tears, & that was to be avoided. I'm glad I said at least one word to you however. I can't tell you what extravagance I have uttered in my heart & you have been spared. I write this now partly (for once) to relieve my feelings – and partly because you were (or affected to be??) surprised at what I said.

Listen – I love you in the most absolute sense possible. I would do anything for you, be anything you wished me, come to you at any time or place if you wished it even for a moment. I should like to state this categorically since the moment for repeating it may not recur soon. If I thought I stood the faintest chance, *vis à vis de toi*, I would fight and struggle savagely. As it is – there are not only the barriers between us of marriage, language, la Manche and doubtless others – there is also the fact that you don't need me in the way in which I need you – which is proved by the amount of time you are prepared to devote to me while I am in Paris. As far as I am concerned this is, *d'ailleurs*, an old story – when you said to me once, *recommençons un peu plus haut*, it was already too late for me to do anything of the kind.

(I wrote thus far in a somewhat proletarian joint in the Rue du Four, when a drunken female put her arm round me *et me demandait si j'ecrivais à maman. J'ai dit que non. Alors elle m'a demandé à qui?* and I didn't know how to reply.)

I don't want to trouble you with this – or rather, not often! I know how painful it is to receive this sort of letter, how one says to oneself oh my God! And turns over the page. I can certainly live without you – it's necessary, and what is necessary is possible, which is just as well. But what I write now expresses no momentary Parisian mood but simply where I stand. You know yourself what it is for one person to represent for another <u>an</u> <u>absolute</u> – and so you do for me. I don't think about you all the time. But I know that there is nothing I wouldn't give up for you if you wanted me. I'm glad to say this (<u>remember</u> <u>it</u>) in case you should ever feel in need of an absolute devotion. (Tho' I know, again, from my own experience, how in a moment of need one is just as likely to rely on someone one met yesterday.)

Don't be distressed. To say these things takes a weight from my heart. The tone dictated to me by your letters *depuis des années me convient peu*. I don't know you quite well enough to know if this is *voulu* or not. Just as I wasn't sure about your 'surprise' on the bridge.

To see you in this impersonal way in Paris, sitting in cafés & knowing you will be gone in an hour, is a supplice. But I well understand & am (I suppose) prepared to digest it, that there is no alternative. If I thought that you would be pleased to see me in Sienna I should come. But (especially after writing to you like this) there is very little possibility of my being able to discover whether you would be pleased or not.

[. . .]

It's happened to me once, twice, perhaps three times in my life to feel an <u>unconditional</u> devotion to someone. The other recipients have gone on their way. You remain. There is no substitute for this sort of sentiment & no mistaking it when it occurs. If it does nothing else, it shows up the inferior imitations.

I wish I could give you something. If anything comes of this novel (or its successor), it's all yours – as is everything else I have if you would. I love you, I love you absolutely and unconditionally – thank God for being able to say this with the whole heart.

I feel reluctant to close this letter because I know that I shan't feel so frank later on. Not that my feelings will have altered, *ça ne change pas*, but I shall feel more acutely the futility at these sort of exclamations. At this moment I am, *même malgré toi*, in communication with you in a way which may not be repeated. If your letters to me could be slightly less impersonal I should be glad. *Mais ça ne se choisit pas.* I have become used to writing impersonally too, & this was a mistake. My dear. It happens to me so rarely to be able to write a letter so wholeheartedly – almost the last but one was a letter I wrote to you in 1946. I love you as much as then. More, because of the passage of time.

Forgive what in this letter is purely 'tiresome'. Accept what you can. If there is anything here which can give you pleasure or could in any bad moment give you comfort I should be very happy. I love you so deeply that I can't help feeling that it must 'touch' you somehow, even without your knowing it. Again, don't be distressed. There is so much I should like to have said to you, & may one day. I don't want to stop writing – I feel I'm leaving you again. My very very dear Queneau –

I

London
Underground
Sept 18

Well, I am back in this delightful sober country again, where politicians are fairly honest & there is no inflation & people behave in a quiet & sensible manner. I am not very pleased, but I shall be happy when I have done some work, which will be about next Friday. I am going to Oxford on Wednesday, as working in London is impossible, and I want to get settled down. [. . .]

I'm sorry about the state I was in in Paris. I could offer several explanations, but what the hell. You are such an old friend now & such a dear one that I shall expect you to put up with such things from time to time & take it as all in the day's work. I'm sorry though. I felt such despair suddenly at the way one brushes past people in life & never really knows them. That maybe one will pass one's whole life without ever having . . . known this person properly, done that thing, been to that place, written the novel one wanted to write . . . very mortal I felt all of a sudden in Paris. (The quartier St Germain is hard on the nerves anyway, don't you think? I found that chance encounters with people would upset me there in a way I can't remember being upset in since Oxford days.)

I'll probably be in Paris in the spring with my mother, who is Romantic, & has never been to France. I want to show her Paris some day. I shall be very sensible then tho'. Some fever has been stilled or at least transformed. Since I have been to Rome & have wept on your shoulder nothing will ever be the same again. Have you been to Rome? [. . .]

I must start work, then all will be well. Write to me soon, please, & tell me how you liked Italy. Very much love to you,
Raymond –
From I

14 Jan 1954
St Anne's College
Oxford

Dear Raymond,

Thank you very much for your New Year card . . . such a
piercing reminder of Paris, oh dear! I was glad to hear from
you.

Listen. I've been meaning to ask you this for some time.
Chatto and Windus will be publishing a novel of mine later
this year – and in accordance with my vow and promise of long
ago I should like to dedicate it to you. I had thought of keeping
quiet about this & just surprising you with the dedication & the
novel together – but then I decided that it's better to warn you,
in case, for any strange reason, you might feel embarrassed or
made in any way uneasy by this offering. I very much hope
you won't be – and that you'll accept it. This would please me
very much. It would bind up many things from my past life
which are important to me. You are connected with nearly
all my early aspirations as a writer – and this book has certain
affinities with *Pierrot*. And apart from all this, I just want very
much to give it to you.

(Whether you'll <u>like</u> it, heaven only knows!)

I'd meant to write at greater length now . . . but it's
beginning of term and I'm in a frenzy of philosophy. I hope
your work goes well, and that you are well . . .

So, my dear Raymond, so . . .
as ever, most affectionately
Iris

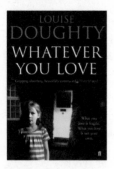

Whatever You Love *Louise Doughty*

A staggering and heart-wrenching new novel from Louise Doughty. Two police officers knock on Laura's door. They tell her that her nine-year old daughter has been hit by a car and killed. When justice is slow, Laura decides to take her own revenge and track down the man responsible, and soon discovers just how far she is prepared to go for love, desire and retribution.

Faber & Faber £12.99

The Last Warner Woman *Kei Miller*

In this tale about magic and migration, a young Jamaican woman with a gift of prophecy embarks on a journey that will take her from a leper colony to revivalist meetings, then to England. This is magical, lyrical and spellbinding writing from the author of the acclaimed *The Same Earth,* described by the *Independent* as 'a name to watch'.

Weidenfeld & Nicolson £12.99

Ilustrado *Miguel Syjuco*

Winner of the Man Asian Literary Prize while still in manuscript form, *Ilustrado* is already a huge literary sensation. On a clear day in winter, the battered corpse of Crispin Salvador is pulled from the Hudson River. Missing, too, is the only manuscript of his final book. His student Miguel must piece together the mystery through fragmented stories covering a generations-long saga of revolution, political intrigue and murder.

Picador

Index on Censorship

International in outlook, outspoken in comment, award-winning magazine *Index on Censorship* is the only publication dedicated to freedom of expression. Its contributors include Nadine Gordimer, Timothy Garton-Ash, Geoffrey Robertson, Ai Weiwei and Jacqueline Rose.

Subscribe to the magazine online for £18 a year, or in print for £28.

Single copies of the new issue are available for £7.99.

Visit www.indexoncensorship.org/subscribe

Losed

This photograph was taken on Memorial Day, 2009, somewhere off Interstate 80 in western Pennsylvania. My sons and I were on a road trip from New York City to the Rock and Roll Hall of Fame in Cleveland, Ohio. Late at night, we took an exit at Sharon and checked into a Holiday Inn. In the morning, it transpired that the Holiday Inn was situated on a hill and that other buildings had been placed on the slope of the hill and in the valley. These included a Subway, a BP gas station, a Staples, a Wal-Mart, a McDonald's and a Video Warehouse. This picture is of the Advanced Auto Parts building.

1:1 – Architects Build Small Spaces

Victoria and Albert Museum – London
15 June – 30 August 2010
www.vam.ac.uk/smallspaces

Study, work, performance, play and contemplation. Explore the work of seven international architects in this specially commissioned series of built spaces. An innovative exhibition of structures that demonstrate the power and possibilities of small spaces and how we use them. Admission free.

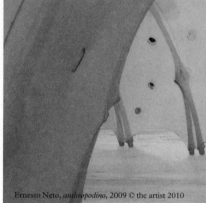

Ernesto Neto:
The Edges of the World

Hayward Gallery – London
19 June – 5 September 2010
www.southbankcentre.co.uk/neto

This summer, dramatic, immersive installations by Ernesto Neto transform the Hayward Gallery's upper galleries. Renowned for his sensuous sculptures, Neto creates site-specific installations evocative of skin and body systems. In this, the artist's most ambitious exhibition in the UK to date, visitors can explore a sequence of interlinked spaces that merge sculpture and architecture.

Ernesto Neto, *anthropodino*, 2009 © the artist 2010

Jeff Kessel and Michelle Segre

North Gallery – New York
July 1 – August 13 2010
www.derekeller.com

For his first solo exhibition in New York, Jeff Kessel will present a series of abstract oil paintings which are made through a process that involves simultaneous control and abandonment and often leads to unforeseen places. In the North Gallery, Michelle Segre will show two new mixed-media sculptures.

TRACES

Ian Teh

The bus from Linfen takes a newly built highway heading south towards the Yellow River. The dust is everywhere, you can feel it on your fingers as something abrasive and dry that you would like to rub away but never can. It coats every surface – from leaves and crops to the buildings and factories lining both sides of the road. It floats in the air creating a fine veil of light yellow that tinges the passing scenery with the same monochromatic hue. A few years ago this would all have been farmland. Now the view is repetitive, rhythmic in its cycles of factories, construction sites and fields of crops with dirt tracks leading deep into the landscape. All available space is used for development or cultivation, crammed into a limited expanse allowing no separation from the factories that produce noxious waste.

In 1999, I read in a newspaper about the contentious Three Gorges Dam project. China's leaders had a grand vision of transforming the Yangtze River into the biggest artificial lake in the world in an attempt to control recurring floods and to generate an estimated 10 per cent increase in energy supply. To achieve this, they would have to resettle 1.5 million people, submerge 13 cities, 400 towns, 1,352 villages, 1,283 archaeological sites and 30,000 hectares of agricultural land.

For four years I made trips to the affected area on the Yangtze River, compiling material for my series *The Vanishing*: *Altered*

Landscapes and *Displaced Lives*. Taking the boat the 700 km from Chongqing to Yichang, I would stop at various ports along the way.

On the one hand there was this grand dream of progress, promoted by the government on billboards along the riverbanks; on the other there was the evident cost of such a grandiose project. Towns once full of life became eerily quiet; occasionally there would be the sound of explosions as buildings were demolished. Migrant labourers armed with sledgehammers, wearing only sandals on their feet, worked till dusk dismantling properties and collecting scrap to sell. Fearful faces would occasionally peer out from half-destroyed homes watching this incredible transformation. These were the unlucky families who had not received compensation – either because of corrupt local bureaucracy or because they had simply fallen through the net. One woman broke down crying when I asked her about her plans. She had moved to Badong after divorcing her husband and supported her two sons by selling tofu that she made in the town market. On the wall of her rented accommodation was a Chinese character in broad red brushstrokes – it said 'dismantle'. Ineligible for compensation because her residential status was for her previous home in another town, and without enough savings to move, she was destitute.

I began to explore the most industrialized regions of China, from the rust belt of the north-east to the cities of Shanxi province, once famous for their coal. In 2007 (the year before the Beijing Olympics), I arrived in Linfen, China's most polluted city. It was just before the week-long Chinese New Year holiday and the government was particularly keen to avoid bad news in the press. For the country's 150 million migrant workers the holiday is especially important; this is the only time they are able to make the long journey home to their families. Miners, construction workers and labourers are mostly migrants from the countryside, the result of two seemingly opposing central government policies. In the late fifties, the household registration system was set up to control internal migration, preceding economic reforms initiated in the late seventies to liberalize the economy. The registration system grants citizens basic rights and social services in their registered home. Workers who leave their home towns or villages lose these rights and become vulnerable to exploitation. They are the lowest-paid social group in China and often work in the most dangerous jobs. Reports of accidents in coal mines and concerns about pollution had attracted media attention and the government took action to avoid any risk of major accidents that could lead to social unrest during the holiday. Many mines and plants that were heavy users of coal were closed down. The sites I visited were often empty, a landscape of dust-coated industrial machinery.

I pursued two simultaneous routes as I compiled images of the coal industry. Both *Traces* and *Tainted Landscapes* explore the other-worldly scenes of the Chinese industrial hinterland, landscapes that seemed to be the repository for all of man's endeavours; a record of our material desires. In contrast, the images that would make up *Dark Clouds* evolved into an intimate chronicle of daily life in these environments. In some images, figures are blurred or distant, anonymous. Others are formal portraits, acknowledging the identity of the individual. These are people forgotten by a society in thrall to the successes of the past two decades: the 'other people' disregarded by the late premier Deng Xiaoping (largely credited for the industrialized China we know today) when he said, 'Let some people get rich first.' Ultimately, the brilliant glare from China's metropolises can be traced back to the hinterland and its migrant workers.

Looking back, I see the dream of a nation, and its cost. A publisher of photography books once said to me that the camera only captured the surface quality of things. At the time I thought it true. But this was accurate only on one level. It is this very limitation that gives the medium its strength. What wasn't said was that we project and give meaning by the way we arrange and edit within the frame; through that we are able to allude to something beyond the immediate. I imagine every story as a woven fabric of compositional and colour threads that come together to create a particular ambience. And yet there should be enough that is left ambiguous to encourage the mind to take the narrative beyond the limits of my frame. ■

TRACES: CHINA 1999 – 2010
Ian Teh

TRACES

TAINTED LANDSCAPES

DARK CLOUDS

THE VANISHING

1999   2010

1. DARK CLOUDS

20. TAINTED LANDSCAPES

39. TRACES

PICTURE CAPTIONS

1. 2008. Polluted river. Datong, Shanxi Province.
2. 2006. Sinter plant. Tonghua, Jilin Province.
3. 2006. Steel workers. Tonghua, Jilin Province.
4. 2007. Coking plant. Benxi, Liaoning Province.
5. 2007. Steel plant. Tonghua, Jilin Province.
6. 2007. A 22-year-old steel worker. Wages: 1000RMB (£73) per month. Tonghua, Jilin Province.
7. 2007. Miner. Linfen, Shanxi Province.
8. 2007. Workers' quarters at a steel plant. Tonghua, Jilin Province.
9. 2006. Over 6,000 Chinese miners die annually in coal mine accidents. Datong, Shanxi Province.
10. 2007. Coking plant. Benxi, Liaoning Province.
11. 2006. Miner plays pool after work. Taiyuan, Shanxi Province.
12. 2007. Snow and fly ash mix on the grounds of a steel plant. Benxi, Liaoning Province.
13. 2006. Chinese miners have the highest rates of respiratory illnesses in the world. Datong, Shanxi Province.
14. 2006. Migrant labourer in a state-owned mine. Datong, Shanxi Province.
15. 2006. Migrant workers. Datong, Shanxi Province.
16. 2006. Lao Liu, miner aged sixteen. Datong, Shanxi Province.
17. 2007. Coking plant. Benxi, Liaoning Province.
18. 2007. Communal bath. Linfen, Shanxi Province.
19. 2007. A tar refinery belches flames, covering the ground with ash and dust. Linfen, Shanxi Province.
20. 2007. The birth of a coal power station. At the time, China was on track to build the equivalent of one power station every week for the next eight years. Tonghua, Jilin Province.
21. 2007. A ventilation system for a power plant at a worker's compound. Tonghua, Jilin Province.
22. 2007. Villagers pass a new cooling tower. Tonghua, Jilin Province.

23. 2007. Assembling a crane at a new power station. Tonghua, Jilin Province.
24. 2007. A mural depicts a famous waterfall on the outskirts of one of the most polluted cities in the world. Linfen, Shanxi Province.
25. 2007. Slag heap dumped near a river. Linfen, Shanxi Province.
26. 2007. Coal reserves at a coking plant. Linfen, Shanxi Province.
27. 2007. Crops near a dirt track by a power plant. Linfen, Shanxi Province.
28. 2003. Settlers from the new city walk home. The old city has been razed and the land reclaimed to protect it from the rising waters. Further up a strip of buildings signifies the start of the new city. Fuling District.
29. 2002. A bridge, once the defining landmark, now weeks away from being destroyed. Wenzhou, Zhejiang Province.
30. 1999. Old passenger boat on the Yangtze River. Chongqing Municipality.
31. 2003. Migrants arrive at the Three Gorges Dam site. Yichang, Hubei Province.
32. 2002. Last inhabitants. Badong, Hubei Province.
33. 2001. Displaced family relocating by boat to the Eastern provinces. Hubei Province.
34. 2003. Locals visiting the newly built docks which are soon to be flooded. Fuling District.
35. 2003. One of the last remaining families, in a once busy city centre, relocates. Wushan.
36. 2010. Industrial tailings. Wuhai, Inner Mongolia, China.
37. 2010. Construction site. Linfen, Shanxi Province.
38. 2010. Ash, industrial tailings and a waste pond blend into the surrounding landscape. Wuhai, Inner Mongolia, China.
39. 2010. Partially demolished steel plant. Hancheng, Shaanxi Province.
40. 2010. The Kuye River, nearly dry from regional over-mining. The city regularly suffers water shortages. Yulin, Shaanxi Province.
41. 2010. A retired truck driver tells me, 'Nothing that is made in this region stays in China. Our government has exported our blue skies to the West.' Wuhai, Inner Mongolia, China.

THE MAGAZINE OF NEW WRITING

GRANTA.COM/US111

PROPERTY

Elizabeth McCracken

The ad should have said, *For rent, six-room hovel. Quarter-filled Mrs Butterworth's bottle in living room, sandy sheets throughout, lingering smell.*

Or, *Wanted: gullible tenant for small house, must possess appreciation for chipped pottery, mid-1960s abstract silk-screened canvases, mouse-nibbled books on Georgia O'Keeffe.*

Or, *Available June 1 – shithole.*

Instead, the posting on the website called the house at 55 Bayberry Street old and characterful and sunny, furnished, charming, on a quiet street not far from the college and not far from the ocean. Large porch; separate artist's studio. Not bad for the young married couple, then, Stony Badower and Pamela Graff, he thirty-nine, red-headed, soft-bellied, long-limbed and beaky, a rare and possibly extinct waterbird; she blonde and soft and hot-headed and German and sentimental. She looked like the plump-cheeked naughty heroine of a German children's book having just sawed off her own braids with a knife. Her expression dared you to teach her a lesson. Like many sentimentalists, she was estranged from her family. Stony had never met them.

'America,' she said that month. 'All right. Your turn. Show me America.' For the three years of their courtship and marriage they'd moved every few months. Berlin, Paris, Galway, near Odense, near Edinburgh, Rome, and now a converted stone barn in Normandy that on cold days smelled of cowpats and on hot days like the lost crayons of tourist children. Soon enough it would be summer and the barn would be colossally expensive and filled with English people. Now it was time for Maine, where Stony had accepted a two-year job, cataloguing a collection of 1960s underground publications: things printed on rice paper and Popsicle sticks and cocktail napkins. It fell to him to find the next place to live.

'We'll unpack my storage space,' he said. 'I have things.'

'Yes, my love,' she said. 'I have things too.'

'You have a duffel bag. You have clothing. You have a salt shaker shaped like a duck with a chipped beak.'

She cackled a very European cackle, pride and delight in her ownership of the lustreware duck, whose name was Trudy. 'The sole exhibit in the museum. When I am dead, people will know nothing about me.' This was a professional opinion: she was a museum consultant. In Normandy she was helping set up an exhibition in a stone cottage that had been owned by a Jewish family deported during the war. In Paris, it had been the atelier of a minor artist who'd been the long-time lover of a major poetess; in Denmark, a workhouse museum. Her speciality was the air of recent evacuation: you knew something terrible had happened to the occupants, but you hoped it might still be undone. She set contemporary spectacles on desktops and snuggled appropriate shoes under beds and did not over-dust. Too much cleanliness made a place dead. In Rome she arranged an exhibit of the commonplace belongings of Ezra Pound: chewed pencils, drinking glasses, celluloid dice, dog-eared books. Only the brochure suggested a connection to greatness. At the Hans Christian Andersen House in Odense, where they were mere tourists, she lingered in admiration over Andersen's upper plate and the length of rope that he travelled with in his suitcase in case of hotel fire. 'You can tell more from dentures than from years of diaries,' she'd said then. 'Dentures do not lie.' But she herself threw everything out. She did not want anyone to exhibit even the smallest bit of her.

Now Stony said, solemnly, 'I never want to drink out of Ikea glasses again. Or sleep on Ikea sheets. Or – and this one is serious – cook with Ikea pans. Your husband owns really expensive pans. How about that?'

'I am impressed, and you are bourgeois.'

'Year lease,' he said.

'I am terrified,' said Pamela, smiling with her beautiful angular un-American teeth, and then, 'Perhaps we will afford to have a baby.'

She was still, as he would think of it later, casually alive. In two months she would be, according to the doctors, *miraculously* alive, and, later still, alive in a nearly unmodifiable twilight state. Or too modifiable: *technically* alive. Now she walked around the barn in her bra, which was as usual a little too small, and her underpants, as usual a little too big, though she was small-breasted and big-bottomed. Her red-framed glasses sat on her face at a tilt. 'My ears are not plumb,' she always said. It was one of the reasons they belonged together: they were flea-market people, put together out of odd parts. She limped. Even her name was pronounced with a limp, the accent on the second syllable. For a full month after they met he'd thought her name was Camilla, and he never managed to say it aloud without lining it up in his head beforehand – paMILLa, paMILLa – the way he had to collect German words for sentences ahead of time and then properly distribute the verbs. In fact he did that with English sentences, too, when speaking to Pamela, when she was alive.

He emailed the woman who'd listed the house – she was not the owner, she was working for the owners – and after a month of wrangling (she never sent the promised pictures; he was third in line, behind a gaggle of students and a clutch of summer people; if they rented for the summer they could make a lot more money), managed to talk her out of a year-long lease, starting June 1.

The limp, it turned out, was the legacy of a stroke Pamela'd had in her early twenties that she'd never told him about. She had another one in the barn two weeks before they were supposed to move; she hit her head on the metal counter as she fell. Stony's French was good enough only to ask the doctors how bad things were, but not to understand the answer. Pamela spoke the foreign languages; he cooked dinner, she proclaimed it delicious. In the hospital her tongue was fat in her mouth and she was fed through a tube. Someone had put her glasses on her face so that she would look more herself. A nurse came in hourly to straighten them. They did this as though her glasses were the masterpiece and all of Pamela the gallery wall

– palms flat and gentle, leery of gravity. He sat in a moulded green chair and dozed. One night he woke to the final nurse, who was straightening the glasses and then the bed sheets. She turned to Stony. The last little bit of French he possessed drained out through the basin of his stomach.

'No?' he said.

This nurse was a small brown rabbit. Even her lips were brown. She wobbled on her feet as though deciding whether it would be better if the mad husband caught and ate her now, or there should be a chase. Then she shrugged.

When someone dies it is intolerable to be shrugged at. He went back to the barn to pack. First his suitcase, an enormous green nylon item with fretful, overworked zippers. Then Pamela's, that beige strap-covered duffel bag that looked like a mid-century truss. He had to leave France as soon as possible. He stuffed the bag with the undersized bras and oversized pants, her favourite pair of creased black patent-leather loafers, an assortment of embroidered handkerchiefs. He needed a suitcase and a computer bag and then any number of plastic bags to move from place to place, he collected souvenirs like vaccinations, but all of Pamela's belongings fit in her bag. When he failed to find the duck, he remembered the words of the lovely Buddhist landlady in Edinburgh, when he'd apologized for breaking a bowl: 'We have a saying – it was already broken.' Even now he wasn't sure if *we* meant Buddhists or Scots. He would leave a note for the landlady concerning the duck, but of course the loss of the duck could not break his heart.

The weight of the bag was like the stones in a suicide's pocket. Stony emailed his future boss, the kindly archivist, asked if he could straighten things out with the real estate agent – he would come, he would definitely come, but in the fall. *My wife has died*, he wrote, in rotten intelligible English. He'd wept already, and for hours, but suddenly he understood that the real thing was coming for him soon, a period of time free of wry laughter or distraction. The bag he put in the closet for the French landlady to deal with. The ashes from the mortuary came in an urn, complete with a certificate that explained what he was to show to customs officials. These he took with him to England, where he went for the summer, to drink.

The Not Owner of the house was a small, slightly creased pony-tailed blonde woman in a baseball cap and a gleaming black exercise suit that suggested somewhere a husband dressed in the exact same outfit. She waved at him from the front porch. For the past month she'd sent him cheerful emails about getting the lovely house ready for him, all of which came down to this: What did he need? What did he own?

Books, art, cooking equipment. And a collection of eccentric but unuseful tables. That was it. He'd chosen this house because it was not a sabbatical rental: even before – a word he now pronounced as a spondee, like BC – he'd longed to be reunited with his books, art, dishes, the doctor's table, the old diner table, the various card catalogues, the side table made from an old cheese crate. He didn't want to live inside someone else's life, and sabbatical houses were always like that. You felt like a teenager who'd been given too much responsibility. Your parents were there frowning at you in the very arrangement of the furniture.

The house wasn't Victorian, as he'd for some reason assumed, but an ordinary wood-framed house painted toothpaste blue. Amazing, how death made petty disappointments into operatic insults.

'Hello!' The woman whooshed across toward him. 'I'm Carly. You're here. At last! It seems like ages since we started talking about you and this house!'

The porch was psoriatic and decorated with a series of lawn chairs.

'I'm glad you found summer people,' said Stony.

Carly nodded. 'Yes. The last guy moved out this morning.'

'Ah,' said Stony, though they'd discussed this via email over the last week. It was his ingratiating way, as a lifelong renter, to suggest unnecessary, helpful things, and he had said he'd arrive on the 4th instead of the 3rd so she'd have more time to arrange for cleaners.

'Fireplace,' she said. 'Cable's still hooked up. Maybe you'll be lucky and they won't notice.' A round-jawed teenager sat on a leather settee with a hand-held video game, frowning at the screen like a Roman emperor impatient with the finickiness of his lions. 'It's a nice room. These old houses have such character. This one – do you believe it? – it's a Sears Roebuck kit. You picked it out of the catalogue and it was delivered and assembled.'

He could hear Pamela's voice: this is not an old house. The barn in Normandy was eighteenth-century, the apartment in Rome even older. The walls were lined with home-made bookshelves, filled with paperback books: Ionesco, the full complement of Roths.

'Fireplace work?'

'There was a squirrel incident,' said Carly vaguely. She swished into the dining room. 'Dining room. The lease, I'm sure you'll remember, asks you to keep the corner cupboard locked.'

The cupboard in question looked filled with eye cups and egg cups and moustache cups. In the corner, a broken styrofoam cooler had been neatly aligned beneath a three-legged chair; a white melamine desk had papers stuck in its jaw. Kmart furniture, he thought. Well, he'd have the movers take it down to the basement.

'Kitchen's this way.'

The kitchen reminded him of his 1970s childhood, and the awful taste of tongue depressors at the back of the throat. It looked as though someone had taken a potting shed and turned it inside out. A pattern of faux shingles crowned the honey-coloured cupboards; the countertop Formica was patterned like a hospital gown. A round, fluorescent light fixture lit up a collection of dead bugs. High above everything, a terracotta sun smiled down from the shingles with no sense of irony, or shame, whatsoever.

The smell of Febreze came down the stairs, wound around the smell of old cigarettes and something chemical, and worse.

'Four bedrooms,' said Carly.

She led him up the stairs into one of the front rooms, furnished with a double mattress on a brown wooden platform. It looked like the sort of thing you'd store a kidnapped teenage girl underneath. The cafe curtains on the windows were badly water-stained and lightly cigarette-burned.

'Listen!' said Carly. 'It's a busy street, but you can't even hear it! Bedclothes in the closets. I need to get going,' she said. 'Tae kwon do. Settle in and let me know if there's anything else I can do for you, all right?'

He had not stood so close to a woman all summer, at least not while sober. He wanted to finger her ponytail and then yank on it like a schoolyard bully.

'Can I see the artist's studio?' he asked.

'Forgot!' she said. 'Come along.'

They walked through the scrubby backyard to a half-converted garage.

'Lock sticks,' said Carly, jiggling a door with a rice-paper cataract over its window. 'Looks dark in here till you turn on the lights.'

The art studio was to have been Pamela's: she was a sometime jeweller and painter. Stony did not know whether it made things better or worse that this space was the most depressing room he'd ever seen. The old blinds seemed stitched together from moth wings. A picture of Picasso, clipped from a newspaper, danced on a bulletin board to a smell of mildew that was nearly audible. Along one wall a busted door rested on sawhorses, and across the top a series of shapes huddled together as though for warmth. Pots, vases, bowls, all clearly part of the same family, the bluish grey of expensive cats. He expected them to turn and blink at him.

'My father was a potter,' said Carly.

It took him a moment. 'Ah! Your parents own this place?'

'My mom,' said Carly. 'She's an ob/gyn. Retired. She's in New York now. You can't go anywhere in this town without meeting kids my mother delivered. She's like an institution. There's a wheel, if you're interested. Think it still works. Potter's.'

'No, thank you.'

She sighed and snapped off the light. They went back to the house. 'All right, pumpkin,' she said, and the teenager stood up and revealed herself to be a girl, not a boy, with a few sharp, painful-looking pimples high on her cheeks, a long nose, and a smile that suggested that not everything was right with her. She shambled over to her tiny mother and the two of them stood with their arms around each other.

Was she awkward, just? Autistic? Carly reached up and curled a piece of hair behind her daughter's ear. It was possible, thought Stony, that all American teenagers might appear damaged to him these days, the way that all signs in front of fast-food restaurants – MAPLE CHEDDAR COMING SOON! McRIB IS BACK – struck him as mysterious and threatening.

'You OK?' Carly asked.

The girl nodded and cuddled closer. The air in the Sears Roebuck house – yes, he remembered now, that was something he would normally be intrigued by, a house built from a kit – felt tender and sad. My wife has died, he thought. He wondered whether Carly might say something. Wasn't now the time? *By the way, I'm sorry. I'm so sorry, what happened to you.* He had that thought sometimes these days. It wasn't grief, which he could be subsumed in at any moment, which like water bent all straight lines and spun whatever navigational tools he owned into nonsense – but a rational, detached thought: wasn't that awful, what happened to me, one, two, three months ago? That was a terrible thing for a person to go through.

Carly said, 'Tae kwon do. Call if you need me.'

An empty package of something called Teddy Lasker. A half-filled soda bottle. Q-tips strewn on the bathroom floor. Mrs Butterworth's, sticky, ruined, a crime victim. Cigarette butts in one window well. Three condom wrappers behind the platform bed. Rubber bands in every drawer and braceleting every doorknob – why were old rubber bands so upsetting? The walls upstairs bristled with pushpins and the ghosts of pushpins and the square-shouldered shadows of missing posters. Someone had emptied several boxes of mothballs into the bedclothes that were stacked in the closets, and had thrown dirty bedclothes on top, and the idea of sorting through clean and dirty made him want to weep. The bath mat looked made of various flavours of old chewing gum. Grubby pencils lolled on desktops and in coffee mugs and snuggled along the baseboards. The dining-room tablecloth had been painted with scrambled egg and then scorched. The walls upstairs were bare and filthy; the walls downstairs covered in old art. The bookshelves were full. On the edges in front of the books were coffee rings and – there was no other word for it – detritus: part of a broken key ring, more pencils, half-packs of cards. He had relatives like this. When he was a kid he loved their houses because of how nothing ever changed, how it could be 1974 outside and 1936 inside, and then he got a little older and realized that it was the same Vicks VapoRub on the bedside table, noticed how once a greetings card was stuck on a dresser mirror it would never be moved, understood that the jars of pennies did not represent possibility, as he'd imagined, but only jars and only pennies.

The landlords had filled the house with all their worst belongings and said: *This will be fine for other people.* A huge snarled antique rocker sat under an Indian print; the TV cart was fake wood and slightly broken. The art on the walls – posters, silk-screened canvases – had been faded by the sun, but that possibly was an improvement.

The kitchen was objectively awful. Old bottles of oil with the merest skim at the bottom crowded the counters. Half-filled boxes of a particularly cheap brand of biscuit mix had been sealed shut with packing tape. The space beneath the sink was filled, back to front, with mostly empty plastic jugs for cleaning fluids. After he opened the kitchen garbage can and a cloud of flies flew out, he called Carly from his newly-purchased cellphone. Her voice was cracked with disappointment.

'Well, I can come back and pick up the garbage –'

'The house,' said Stony, 'is dirty. It's dirty. You need to get cleaners.'

'I don't think Mom will go for that. She paid someone to clean in May –'

Pamela would have said, *Walk out*. Sue for the rent and the deposit. That is, he guessed she would. Then he was furious that he was conjuring up her voice to address this issue.

'The point,' he said, 'is not that it was clean in May. It's not clean now. It's a dirty house, and we need to straighten this out.'

'I have things I have to do,' said Carly. 'I'll come over later.'

Then the movers arrived, two men who looked like middle-aged yoga instructors. The boss exuded a strange calm that seemed possibly like the veneer over great rage. He whistled at the state of the house, and Stony wanted to hug him.

'Don't lose your cool,' said the mover. 'Hire cleaners. Take it out of the rent.'

They unloaded all of Stony's old things: boxes of books, boxes of dishes, all the things he needed for his new life as a bourgeois widower. He really lived here. He felt pinned down by the weight of his belongings and then decided it was not a terrible feeling. From the depths of his email program he dug up an email from Carly that cc'd Sally Lasker, to whom he'd written the rent cheque. If he sat on the radiator at the back of the room and leaned, he could catch just a scrap of a wireless connection, and so he sat, and leaned, and wrote what seemed to him a firm but sympathetic email to Sally Lasker, detailing everything but her unfortunate taste in art.

Sally wrote back:

> We cleaned the house in May, top to bottom. It took me a long time to dust the books, I did it myself. I cleaned the coffee rings off the bookcase. We laundered all the bedclothes. I'm sorry that the house is not what you expected. I'm sorry that the summer people have caused so much damage. That can't have been pleasant for you. But it seems that you are asking a great deal for a nine-month rental. We lived modestly all our lives, I'm afraid, and perhaps this

is not what you pictured from Europe. I do feel as though we have
bent over backwards for you so far.

He went over this in a confused rage. What difference did it make
that the house was clean in May? That there had been coffee rings
before where coffee rings were now? He'd turned forty over the
summer and it reminded him of turning eighteen. *I am not a child!* he
wanted to yell. *I do not sleep on home-made furniture! I do not hide filthy
walls with posters and Indian hangings!*

What did she mean, bent over backwards?

He stalked into the sweet little Maine town and had two beers in
a sports bar, then stalked back. All the while he wrote to Sally in his
head, and told her he was glad she'd found summer renters who'd
made up the rent and maybe she had not heard what exactly had
delayed his arrival.

When he found the wireless again, there was a new email:

> Hire the cleaners. Take the total out of the rent. I am sorry,
> and I hope this is the end of the problems. If you want to store
> anything precious, put it in the studio, not the basement. The
> basement floods.

So he couldn't even send his righteous email.

That night he boxed up Sally's kitchen and took it to the
basement, pulled the art from the walls and put it in the dank
studio. He couldn't decide on what was a more hostile act, packing
the filthy bath mat or throwing it away. Packing it, he decided, and
so he packed it. He tumbled the mothball-filled bedclothes into
garbage bags. He moved out the platform bed and slept on the futon
sofa and went the next day to the nearby mall to buy his very own
bed. The following Monday the cleaners came, looking like a *Girls
in Prison* movie (missing teeth, tattoos, denim shorts, cleavage) and
declared without prodding that the house was disgusting, and he felt
a small surge of actual happiness: yes, disgusting, it was, anyone
could see it. He was amazed at how hard they worked. They cleaned
out every cupboard. They hauled all those bottles to the curb. He

tipped them extravagantly. One of the cleaners left her number on several pieces of paper around the house – PERSONAL HOUSE-CLEANING CALL JACKIE $75 – and the owner of the cleaning service called the next day to say that she'd heard one of the girls was offering to clean privately, was that true, it wasn't allowed, and Stony accidentally said yes, and was heartbroken, that the perfect transaction of cleaning had been ruined. Then he called back and said he'd misunderstood, she hadn't. Everything had been perfect.

That night he wrote Sally an email explaining where everything was: kitchen goods boxed in basement, linens and art in the studio.

He painted the upstairs walls and hung his own art. He boxed up some of the books. Slowly he moved half the furniture to the studio and replaced it with things bought at auction. The kindly archivist, his boss, came by the house.

'My God!' he said. 'This place! You've made it look great. You know, I tried to get you out of the lease last May, but Sally wouldn't go for it. I tried to find you someplace nicer. But you've made it nice. Good for you.'

At work he catalogued the underground collection, those beautiful daft objects of passion, pamphlets and buttons, broadsides. What would the founders of these publications make of him? What pleasure, to describe things that had been invented to defy description – but maybe he shouldn't have. The inventors never imagined these things lasting forever, filling phase boxes, the phase boxes filling shelves. He was a cartographer, mapping the unmappable, putting catalogue numbers and provenance where once had been only waves and the profiles of sea serpents. Surely some people grieved for those sea serpents.

He didn't care. He kept at it, constructing his little monument to impermanence.

By March he was dating a sociology lecturer named Eileen, a no-nonsense young woman who made comforting, stodgy casseroles and gave him back rubs. He realized he would never know what his actual feelings for her were. She was not a girlfriend; she was a side effect of everything in the world that was Not Pamela. The house, too. Every now and then he thought, out of the blue: But what did that woman mean, she bent over backwards for me? And all day long, like a telegraph, he received the following message: *My wife has died, my wife has died, my wife has died.* Quieter than it had been; he could work over it now. He could act as though he were not an insane person with one single thought.

In April he got a tattoo at a downtown parlour where the students got theirs, a piece of paper wafting as though windswept over his bicep with a single word in black script: *Ephemera.*

Then it was May. His lease was over. Time to move again.

Through some spiritual perversity, he'd become fond of the house: its Sears Roebuck feng shui, its square squatness, the way it got light all day long. Sally sent him emails, dithering over move-out dates, and for a full week threatened to renew the lease for a year. Would he be interested? He consulted his heart and was astounded to discover that yes, he would. Finally she decided she would move back to the house on June 1st to get it ready to sell. Did he want to buy it? No, ma'am. Well then: May 30th.

He found an apartment with a bit of ocean view, a grown-up place with brand-new appliances and perfect arctic countertops that reminded him of no place: not the stone barn in Normandy, nor the beamed Roman apartment, nor the thatched cottage near Odense. As he packed up the house he was relieved to see its former grubbiness assert itself, like cleaning an oil painting to find a murkier, uglier oil painting underneath. He noticed the acoustic tiles on the upstairs ceilings and the blackness of the wooden floors. He took up the kilim he'd put down in the living room and replaced the old oriental; he packed his flat-screen TV, a splurge, into a box and found in the basement the old mammoth remoteless TV and the hobbled particle-board cart. He cleaned the house as he'd never cleaned before, because he was penitent and because he suspected Sally would use any opportunity to hold on to his security deposit; he washed walls and the insides of cupboards and baseboards and door jambs. She had no idea how much work she had ahead of her, he thought. The old rocker was a pig to wrestle back into the house; he covered it with the Indian throw, so she would have someplace to sit, but he left the art off the walls, and he did not restock the kitchen, because that would have made more work for her.

And besides.

Besides, why should he?

Those boxes were time machines: if he even thought about them, all he could remember was the fury with which he packed them. These days he was pretending to be a nice, rational man.

He bought a bunch of daffodils and left them in a pickle jar in the middle of the dining-room table with a note that reminded Sally of the location of her kitchenware and bedlinen, and signed his name, and added his cellphone number. Then he went away for the weekend, up the coast, so he could take a few days off from things, boxes, the fossil record of his life.

In the morning, the first cellphone message was Sally, who wanted to know where her dishcloths were.

The second: bottom of the salad spinner.

The third: her birth certificate. She'd left it in the white desk that had been in the dining room and where was that?

The fourth: what on earth had happened to the spices? Had he put them in a separate box?

The reception in this part of the state was miserable. He clamped the phone over one ear and his hand over the other.

'Sally?' he said.

She said, 'Who's this?'

'Stony Badower.'

There was silence.

'Your tenant –'

'I know,' she said, in a grand-dame voice. Then she sighed.

'Are you all right?' he asked.

'It's been more daunting moving back in than I'd thought,' she said.

'But you're all right.'

'I found the dishcloths,' she said. 'And the desk.'

'And the birth certificate?' he asked.

'Yes.' More silence.

'Why don't I come over this evening when I get back,' he said, 'and I can –'

'Yes,' she said. 'That would be nice.'

He'd imagined a woman who looked spun on a potter's wheel, round and glazed and built for neither beauty nor utility. Unbreakable till dropped from a height. But the door was answered by a woman as tall as him, five feet ten, in her late sixties, more ironwork than pottery, with the dark hair and sharp nose of her granddaughter. She shook his hand. 'Stony, hello.' Over a flowered T-shirt she wore the sort of babyish bright blue overalls that Berlin workmen favoured, that no American grown-up would submit to (or so he'd have thought). They showed off the alarmingly beautiful small of her back as she retreated to the kitchen. Already she'd dug out some of the old pottery and found a new tablecloth to cover the cigarette-burned oilcloth on the dining-room table.

'What I don't understand . . .' she said.

In each hand as she turned was a piece of a salad spinner: the lid with the cord that spun it like a gyroscope, the basket that turned. Her look described the anguish of the missing plastic bowl with the point at the bottom. His own salad spinner was waiting in a box in the new apartment. It worked by a crank.

'Who packed the kitchen?' she asked.

'I did,' he said.

'What I don't understand,' she said again, 'was that these were in *separate* boxes. And the bottom? Gone.'

'Oh,' he said.

She gestured to the wooden shelf – Murphy's oil-soaped and bare

– by the window. 'What about the spices?'

'That's my fault,' he said, though before he'd come over he'd googled *how long keep spices* and was gratified by the answer. He could see them still, sticky, dusty, greenish-brown grocery-store spice jars, the squat plastic kind with the red tops. He'd thrown them out with everything else that had been half used. 'I got rid of them. They were dirty. Everything in the kitchen was.'

She shook her head sadly. 'I wiped them all down in May.'

'Sally,' he said. 'Really, I promise, the kitchen was dirty. It was so, so filthy.' Was it? He tried to remember, envisioned the garbage can of flies, took heart. 'Everything. It's possible that I didn't take time to pick out exactly what was clean and what wasn't, but that was how bad things were.'

She sighed. 'It's just – I thought I was moving back home.'

'Oh,' he said. 'So – when did you move out?'

'Four years ago. When I retired. Carly grew up here. She didn't tell you? I was always very happy in this house.'

'No,' he said. He'd thought they'd moved ten years ago. Twenty.

'Listen, I have some favours to ask you. If you could help me move some furniture back in.'

'Of course,' he said.

'There's an armchair in the studio I'd like upstairs. So I have something to sit on. I was looking for my bed, you know. That really shouldn't have been moved.'

'I said, I think –'

'It's all right. Amos made it. He made a lot of the furniture here – the shelves, the desks. He was a potter.'

'I'm so sorry,' he said, because after Pamela died, he'd promised himself that if anyone told him the smallest, saddest story, he would answer, *I'm so sorry*. Meaning, *Yes, that happened.* You couldn't believe the people who believed that not mentioning sadness was a kind of magic that could stave off the very sadness you didn't mention – as though grief were the opposite of Rumpelstiltskin, and materialized only at the sound of its own name.

'That asshole,' she said. '*Is* a potter, I should say.' She looked around the kitchen. 'It's just,' she said, 'the bareness. I wasn't expecting that.'

She turned before his eyes from an iron widow into an abandoned wife.

'I figured you were selling the house,' he said.

She scratched the back of her neck. 'Yes. Come,' she said in the voice of a pre-school teacher. 'Studio.'

It was raining and so she put on a clear raincoat, another childish piece of clothing. She even belted it. They went out the back door that Stony had almost never used. In the rainy dusk, the transparent coat over the blue, she looked alternately like an art deco music box and a suburban sofa wrapped against spills.

The doorknob stuck. She pushed it with her hip. 'Can you?' she asked, and he manhandled it open and flicked on the light.

Here it was again: the table covered with pots, Picasso dancing, though now Picasso was covered up to his waist in mould. The smell was terrible. He saw the art he'd brought out nine months before, which he'd stacked carefully but no doubt had been ruined by the damp anyhow. He felt the first flickers of guilt and tried to cover them with a few spadefuls of anger: if it hadn't happened to her things, it would have happened to his.

'Here everything is,' she said. She pointed in the corner. 'Oh, I love that table. It was my mother's.'

'Well, you said not the basement.'

'You were here for only nine months,' she said. She touched the edge of the desk that the blue pots sat on, then turned and looked at him. 'It's a lot to have done, for only nine months.'

She was smiling then, beautifully. Raindrops ran down her plastic-covered bosom. She stroked them away and said, 'When I walked in it just felt as though the twenty-five years of our residency here had been erased.'

Oh, lady, he wanted to say, you rented me a house, a house, not a museum devoted to you and to Laskeriana and the happiness and failure of your marriage. You charged me market rent, and I paid it so I could *live* somewhere. But he realized he'd gotten everything wrong. She had not left her worst things behind four years ago, but her best things, her beloved things. She'd left the art, hoping it would bring beauty into the lives of the students and summer renters and other wayward subletters, all those people unfortunate enough not to have made a home here yet. She loved the terracotta sun that he'd taken down from the kitchen the first day. She loved the bed made for her in the 1970s by that clever, wretched man her husband. She bought herself a cheap salad spinner so her tenants could use this one which worked so well. If Pamela had been with him that day nine months ago, she would have known. She would have seen the pieces of key chain and clucked over the dirty rug and told him the whole story. This was a house abandoned by sadness, not a war or epidemic but the end of a marriage, and kept in place to commemorate both the marriage and its ruin.

'It was such a strange feeling, to see everything gone,' she said. 'As though ransacked. You know?'

He'd never even called the French landlady to ask about Trudy the lustreware duck, and right now that seemed like the biggest lack in his life, worse than Pamela, whom he knew to be no longer on this earth. He should have carried the duck to America, though he'd scattered Pamela's ashes on the broads in Norfolk. He should have flown to Bremen, where she was from, to startle her mother and sisters, demanded to see her childhood bed, tracked it down if it was gone from whatever thrift store or relative it had been sent to – Pamela was the one who taught him that a bed on display is never just furniture, it is a spirit portrait of everyone who has ever slept in it, been born in it, had sex in it, died in it. *Look*, she said. *You can see them if you look.* He had done everything wrong.

'I know,' he said. 'I'm sorry,' he said, and then, 'It was already broken.' ∎

LINO

Colin Grant

It was a big news day. We were going to look for a piece of lino for the back room. At least, that was the plan. Bageye had woken irritably in the morning to a strong reminder from our mother that he'd been promising that this was *the day*. 'You start already?' said Bageye. 'Not even have breakfast and you start already.' He rifled through a kitchen drawer, picked up a knife and began to peel an orange as his wife laid before him the inarguable fact that he couldn't put off buying the lino any longer, especially as the health visitors were coming first thing next week to inspect the house following the arrival of baby G. She finished her piece and waited for him to speak. Bageye concentrated on the orange until all the skin was removed and the unbroken kiss-curl of peel dropped into the bin. She tried again: 'You never hear? The government people did warn you once.' Bageye didn't blink. He took it all in as a newsflash that, until now, had been kept from him. He cut the top off the orange as some people cut the top off a boiled egg. Only when he'd munched his way through the entire orange did I see, through the crack in the door, that he was heading towards us.

Everyone assumed innocent positions on the floor or settee as his head came round the door. His eyes fell on the cracked, degraded lino. He scanned the room for culprits and half muttered to himself, half declaimed, 'Not even six months and dem mash up the t'ing so?' We children were careful not to catch his eye but at the same time trembled at the consequences of being caught looking away. He shouted in our general direction: 'Carry on. You pickney gonna bury me and is bawl you will bawl when dem screw down the coffin lid.' It was already nine o'clock, yet the heavy curtains, Bageye noticed, were not fully drawn, contrary to the rules. It could only mean that something was being hidden. He tugged at the curtains and exposed the crack and pebble-sized hole in the window, above the sill, that had still not been fixed but plugged with newspaper taped to the glass.

A week had passed since that particular catastrophe. Bageye had forgotten about it, but he pulled back now from opening up this new avenue of discontent. He cast his sad bag-eyes over his offspring and singled me out to keep him company on the journey he was suddenly determined to make. He turned to those who'd be left behind: 'And nah bother long down your mout'.'

Bageye mistook the sour faces of my brothers and sisters for disappointment when really their expressions were designed to put him off choosing them. I hadn't yet perfected the look. My father favoured me, because, as he often declared to the others, even though I was only ten: 'that boy is a common-sense man'. I was told to run a comb through my head and put some shine on my shoes, quick-time. Bageye, meanwhile, adjusted his paisley scarf – he wore it like an English gentleman – and put on his brown corduroy cap, telling anyone who cared to listen: 'When you don't see me, I'm gone.' You had to admit the man had style.

We never addressed our father as Bageye. That was a pet name given him by the fellas. The legend was obscure to us. Only years later did I make the connection with a harmless condition doctors call 'subcutaneous oedema'. Now, looking back, it shouldn't have been the mystery that it was, although no one questioned its origins. He'd had the look from the age of sixteen or thereabouts, apparently. Once the bags first appeared under his eyes as a young galley boy at sea, it wasn't long before some wag had christened him 'Bageye'. And the name stuck. He could no more change it than he could the colour of his eyes. It was never soft-sounding, and on the wrong teasing lips it carried an added sting. You could tell that Bageye wasn't in love with the name but if he resented it he never said. Everyone had to have a name. Bageye's was probably on a par with 'Pumpkin Head' and 'Anxious'. Each man was reduced to that which was most obvious about him. Some were luckier than others. 'Shine', of course, was bald; 'Pappa Tunce' was an older guy; 'Tidy Boots' was fastidious. Everyone's favourite was 'Summer Wear,' so called because he had come to this country in his light summer suit; he refused to wear heavy winter clothes. Summer Wear was a carefree soul with a sunny disposition but the winter before, dressed as usual in only a short-sleeved shirt and linen trousers, he had caught pneumonia and died. No one was as popular with the men as Summer Wear, but I reckoned that Bageye, despite his name, was a close second. He was like a balloon inflating whenever the fellas came around the house, but the air would soon begin to escape once they'd departed.

Outside, Bageye ran the shammy leather over the roof of the car before he got in, slipping into his favourite spot, behind the wheel. He turned to inspect how I intended to close the passenger-side door. OK, it was only a second-hand Mini-Estate. You might not think much of it, but Bageye didn't work overtime and night shifts at the Electrolux factory just so that us pickney could slam off the door. His scrutiny, though, did pose a slight dilemma because if you pulled the door too gently it wouldn't close properly. And, bwoy, as far as my father was concerned, if you hadn't managed on the second go, then it was best to pretend that you had.

Slide in, close the door firmly, look straight ahead and whatever you do, don't ask where we're going. Those were the essential points to concentrate on. 'Let we check by Bernard first,' said Bageye. It was what he always said when anything, any appliance or furnishing, needed to be replaced. Bernard's junk shop, the Bargain Box, was crammed to the rafters with second-hand treasures. It required some purpose and determination to squeeze through the heavily fortified front door into the cornucopia of goods salvaged from house clearances and pawned items that were never likely to be redeemed. Bernard had not mastered the art of stock-keeping; there was always an imbalance between stock bought by him and that which remained to be sold. A man with a more subtle mind might have felt mocked by the electric fires, rugs and assorted unwanted goods that had taken up permanent residence in Bernard's Bargain Box. Not Bernard. He puffed out his chest with all the proprietorial pride of the owner of an upmarket boutique. But Bageye knew – and you'd be a fool to try tell him any different – that, 'is pure junk inside. Is t'ief Bernard t'ief and one day dem gonna burn down him kiss-me-arse shop.'

There was no way, of course, that we could go straight to Bernard's. Bageye would have to check by a few of his friends first, call in on his spar along the way. I was very well versed in the rules of my father's world, and equally conscious that the rules could change at any time. Just a few minutes into the journey, Bageye wanted to know how his son felt about a piece of carpet instead of the lino. 'Man to man, I'm asking you,' he said.

'Carpet would be nice but . . .' I felt my way to what should have been the right answer, '. . . isn't it too expensive? And surely, lino or carpet, us kids will mash it up the same way.' It was a good response.

'You see your mother? Credit! That woman just love credit. Never know a woman love credit so.' He eased back on the gas, the better to take the subject in his stride. 'A man must pay his bills before he can allow himself the smallest luxury.'

It was no surprise then that we seemed to be heading in the direction of Joe Barnes's. While most of my father's friends, like him, were lean and tidily but modestly built, Joe Barnes had arms that bulged like Popeye's after a can of spinach. He had taken an *Atlas* course and turned out magnificently. But more than his athleticism, it was his generosity that impressed our mother and us kids; only Bageye demurred.

Bageye was still smarting from heroic Joe's latest unwelcome intervention into our lives, dropping off a free bag of corn-on-the-cob at the house a few nights back, when Bageye was on the night shift. The way Bageye saw it, he didn't remember ever asking Joe to bring that stinking sack of corn-on-the-cob to the house in the first place. Though Joe said it was a gift, Bageye shuddered at the shame of his wife letting Joe leave empty-handed. 'Imagine that! How you feel that make me look?' moaned my father. 'A long-seed man like me can't provide food on the table for his pickney?' At this point Bageye demanded to know exactly what my mother had had to say on the matter. He wasn't asking his son to 'carry go, bring come,' to betray any secrets. He just wanted to be sure that she wasn't turning all five pickney against him. It was clear Bageye was only going to ask the once, and I calculated that my mother wouldn't blame me for what I was about to admit. That as far as she was concerned, she didn't understand why, when Bageye had so many pickney hungry, with their shoe-backs breaking down, why he, Bageye, would no doubt end up giving money to Joe Barnes and, worse still, more than Joe had paid for the offending corn-on-the-cob in the first instance. Bageye stopped the car: 'Listen, bwoy, when it comes down to it, remember this: death before dishonour.'

Life was too sweet for Joe Barnes. He had the kind of noble face that looked like it had been chiselled out of a mountain and wavy hair that was all his own, no chemicals applied. Joe was a sweet bwoy, they said, but no sweet-back. His ways were a regular topic of conversation for my father and his spars. It was a risk, but I decided to venture on a little conversation with Bageye, spicing my comments with some of the things I had heard the big men say. What puzzled me about Joe Barnes, I suggested to my father, what I really couldn't work out, was which of the two women that Joe lived with was his wife. They were mother and daughter – each as big as the other. 'Plenty man would like be in Joe position,' is all Bageye would say on the matter. It was true, all the fellas admired Joe. The mother and daughter may have been on the plain side. They may have had big bellies and been a little too fond of cheap perfume, but at the time when Joe took up with them, none of the fellas could even stand at the same bus stop as a white woman.

Joe and his women lived up at High Town in one of those houses where you went from street to front room in one step. Except on this day, there were so many sacks in the front room that we could hardly squeeze in. Each room in the house was full of hemp sacks. The sacks were full of corn-on-the-cob and the smell announced that they were just beginning to turn. Joe was a wheeler-dealer; he was a man who always knew a man who knew a man. Only one man liked to take chances more than Joe and that was Bageye. And when the time came to leave Joe's, I knew that even though we already had enough corn to last us a month, we'd not be leaving empty-handed. Somehow Bageye seemed able to see my mother's disbelief and disdain anticipated in my own face. 'Mek her stay there cuss her bad word,' Bageye said of his wife. 'I know a man, one of my spar, might can do something with this.' I foresaw a future of corn-on-the-cob for breakfast, lunch and dinner and though I never saw the money pass hands, I reckoned there'd be no more discussion about the merits of a carpet over lino.

The business with Joe Barnes was a bad sign. Bageye was in the mood now of the repentant drunk or gambler, suddenly struck by the ennobling idea of settling his debts. If it was his last night on earth, Bageye would have to pay his dues – at least those he could afford.

We pulled up outside the Indian tobacco shop. Mr Maghar was actually from Uganda. But it didn't matter that each morning as a boy Mr Maghar rose at five to feed the goats on the hills of Juba; he was still a clever Bombay Indian who'd sell a man one shoe, as far as my father was concerned. But Bageye was also a practical man and if he had to swallow his pride and ask for credit from a tobacconist, it might as well be from the 'cha-cha' man close to home. For the last week I'd been going, at my father's beckoning, to pick up his Embassy Number 1 and a box of matches from Mr Maghar. As the week progressed, I'd also taken to bringing back a little something for myself as a reward. The one bar of Cadbury's chocolate – just this once – had become a daily routine. I reflected now that it was a strange coincidence because last year it had happened to my brother. His inability to stop rewarding himself had seemed beyond his control, as if he was possessed. And that time when Bageye found out, he had unbuckled his belt. He never liked to do it, so he said, took no pleasure from it, but: 'If pickney can't learn then they will feel – simple so.'

Before leaving me in the car, Bageye warned me, as he always did, not to touch anything. I nodded, but I wasn't really listening. My mind was fixed on the image of my father in conversation with

Maghar, unsuspecting of the size of the bill he was about to receive. I held on to the faint hope that he, somehow, wouldn't notice – a hope that slipped away with every minute of his prolonged absence. It probably wasn't that long. It was like that time I was knocked off my bike and everything appeared to be going in slow motion. I forced myself not to look out of the car window but had no control over ears that strained to hear him returning, trying to work out the menace, the degree of violence in his footsteps. Something told me to run. But where to? I was pulled up by hesitations, each one more sickening than the last. And it was with some relief that I heard the driver-side door open, followed by an unexpected silence. Bageye took an Embassy Number 1 and pressed in the cigarette lighter on the dashboard. While he waited for it to heat up an idea seemed to come to him. When the lighter pinged he held it up. But, by the time he put it to the cigarette, the glow from the filament had dimmed, so he had to press the lighter back into the socket on the dashboard once more. 'If you want sweet, why didn't you come to me and ask?' Bageye spoke suddenly, but quietly. 'Wha'appen? You don't have tongue in your head?' It occurred to me that lately I'd been shedding a lot of tears in front of my father. The truth was I could hold out against anger and violence but was wrong-footed when confronted by gentleness and disappointment. '"Didn't the boy ask your permission?"' Bageye mimicked Mr Maghar. He snorted. 'Is so the man speak to me. "Didn't the boy ask your permission?" You don't hear the slur? I didn't bring up my pickney to take liberty. And no one's going to take liberty with my pickney.' It frightened me that my father was working himself up into a temper, talking about his number-one son as if I wasn't sat there right beside him in the front of the car. It must have been Maghar's doing. Maghar who encouraged the boy to spend more and more. And when it gone too far now . . . Bageye sucked on the idea. He took a polo mint from a near-empty pack and cracked the sweet between his teeth. 'Bet it wasn't even that many chocolate. Expec' one or two extra bar found dem way on to the list, right? Clever Mr Indian t'ink he can use his brains 'pon me. You t'ink I born yesterday? Is forty-eight years ago I born. Mek Maghar stay there lick him chops. Is finish I finish with him tonight.' Tomorrow, Bageye would change his tune. Tomorrow I would have to run and fetch ten Embassy Number 1s or a pack of Marlboro with king-size Rizlas. But tomorrow, from Mr Maghar, I also knew, there would be no fantastic tales of herding sheep on the hills of Juba. Tomorrow, the kindly shopkeeper would hand over the cigarettes in silence and coldly cut his eye after me as I left the shop.

Bageye counted what was left of the money. He stopped and bid me check it for him. Already the notes were few and starting to look grubby. 'Even if I'm down to my last penny, that floor gone cover tonight!' Bageye stressed a little too earnestly. 'But bwoy we take a knock with this sweet business, might have to make do with the lino after all.' He folded the money back into his clip. 'Only one wage coming in and we have to make it stretch.' He counted out thirty pounds and asked me to hold out my hand. 'Squeeze tight. It the lino money. Blood money.'

But if I concluded that we must now be heading to Bernard's, I needed to think again, because Bageye first had to run by Anxious so the two of them could share a smoke. Although 'share' might not have been the most appropriate word. My father liked to smoke in company but he shared a cigarette like he shared a joke; it was mostly for his own enjoyment. His wife might begrudge him the smoke when the cupboard was bare, but the cigarette was the one little pleasure Bageye had. Superkings held much more tobacco than a normal cigarette, and if Bageye could break one up, unpack it into a Rizla, add a little something to make it sweet, roll it again, then he could make it last a whole heap of time. Though I'd heard my mother describe him as 'misery who likes company', Anxious lived alone. He just couldn't seem to hold down a woman, the fellas used to say.

Anxious admired the cigarette as he dragged on the last draw, and I got up on cue, ready to leave. 'Settle back into your seat man,' Bageye said languidly. 'The day long.' And winking at me, he added, 'Let me have ten from that t'ing I give you.' I knew better than to hesitate and handed over ten from the thirty pounds left in my charge. 'Is your son that, Bageye? Him turn big man.' Anxious laid a fat palm on my head. 'So, is Bageye son that.' There was something improper, taunting, in the way he said it. I couldn't figure it out, nor did I understand why he never addressed me directly. 'The boy want something to eat?' It sounded like a threat. Anxious only had a vague memory of how to cook. One time someone had showed him how you could boil up pig-foot to make soup.

'You never hear the man ask you a question?'

It was never clear how Bageye could become irritated so suddenly. He was like an old wound. Knock it and it would flare up. At times, you could be forgiven for thinking he actually resented the fact that children needed food and water. But what he resented more was the thought of Anxious, however innocently, pointing this out. Bageye lifted the lid on the pot and looked in scornfully. 'What this t'ing need is a little something spice it up.'

'You don't see the cupboard empty, Bageye?'

'You don't have no sweetcorn?' asked my father. 'No sweetcorn, no yam and cassava, no callaloo, no nothing. Not a t'ing.' Bageye opened up a succession of bare cupboards filled only with crystallized cobwebs. 'I can't make no promise but there's a chance . . .' He broke off and checked his watch. 'Have to move quick-time. What you say, Anxious? I know a man, one of my spar, can throw three or four sack of sweetcorn your way, and a sweet price.'

Anxious drew back his head the better to suggest surprise: 'Three or four sack!'

'We not dealing with loose change here, you dig?' said Bageye. 'You don't have to eat the whole t'ing. Tek what you need and sell it on, simple so.'

Anxious ran a fat furry tongue slowly along the cigarette paper. 'What am I going to do with three or four sack of sweetcorn? Not even one or two, but three or four?'

'One or two then,' said Bageye. And with that Bageye swept me out of the chair towards the front door. Anxious shouted after us:

'That sweetcorn better be sweet, you hear, Bageye.'

No matter which way he turned on the route back to Joe Barnes's, my father had to drive past Bernard's. He braked sharply outside the Bargain Box. We sat in silence as Bageye turned over the unwelcome thought – *to buy or not to buy the lino* – that my presence had forced upon him.

A bell rang as we stepped inside. We pushed past all the junk at the front of the shop to all the junk at the back. To the unsuspecting eye, Bernard looked like a grey and feeble matchstick man with a cigarette permanently glued to the side of his mouth. But though you might think he was unfit, he was a black-belt and famed as the only man in Luton ever to have made a citizen's arrest, when, on 7 June 1971, some light-fingered fool tried his luck in the shop. The poor man hadn't read the signs. Where other shopkeepers displayed the usual prohibitive placards – *In God We Trust, Everyone Else Pays Cash* – Bernard had simply hung his embossed black-belt certificate on the wall behind the till. The citizen's arrest had made the headlines in the *Luton News* a few years back. Multiple copies of that edition wallpapered the shop. Together with the framed black certificate, they put the more discerning customer on notice that he or she should beware the quality of the man behind the counter.

Bernard held out rolls of lino for Bageye to choose. Each one was worn thin, stained and cracked, and not much better than the one on the floor back at our house. My father was clearly affronted by the quality. 'How much for that one there, on the top shelf?' he asked. Bernard gazed sceptically at my father.

'That one's nearly new.'

'That's not what I asked. Cho' man!' Bageye put out his hand and I passed him the remainder of the money. He slapped the twenty down on the counter. 'Hold this as deposit nah, man. We soon come with the rest.'

Back in the car, Bageye invited me to reflect on the meaning behind the words 'that one's nearly new' again and again. 'You see how the man speak to me? And in front of my pickney!' First Maghar and now Bernard. My father was so *vexed* he could spit: 'I've been among these people long enough to know what strokes they play. Bwoy, it not a good idea to stay in white-man country too long.'

Outside Joe Barnes's yard, my father kept the engine running. He went in and came out in a hurry, returning to the car with two more sacks of corn. Things were moving fast now. In half an hour Bernard's would be shut. We got back to Anxious in good time. Bageye rolled out of the front seat, leaving the car door open. 'Only one more stop after this, little man,' he assured me. For the briefest moment, I saw an expression on his face that I did not, at first recognize. Bageye smiled. My father smiled at me. I told myself to hold on to the memory, to remember to tell the others.

Ten minutes passed before I saw him again. Bageye was not renowned for sharing what was on his mind, but it was all too easy to pick up the bad vibe as he approached. Something had gone horribly wrong. And, if I wasn't mistaken, were there two more fermenting sacks of corn being shoved on to the back seat? Bageye had gone in with the two sacks he'd expected to sell, and returned with them. He almost broke off the car key when he turned the ignition. The deal with Anxious couldn't have gone to plan. The mood he was in now, never mind carpet, you could kiss even the cheapest piece of lino goodbye. 'You can't sit still?' my father barked at me even though I hadn't moved a muscle since he got back in. It was a very bad sign. Worse, now we were heading for home.

Bageye didn't bother to knock, that wasn't his style. He struggled to open the front door with the sacks of corn in his arms. My mother retreated a little, stepped to one side, planted her feet and hissed, 'I'm not saying a word.' She could have screamed it, Bageye paid her no mind. He threw the sacks under the kitchen sink and hurried back towards the front door. 'What about the lino?' The words came despite her pledge, dripping in sarcasm. Bageye turned to his wife and let fly a stream of bad words. He cursed her and then cursed some more. And the curses remained in the air as the front door slammed shut after him. ∎

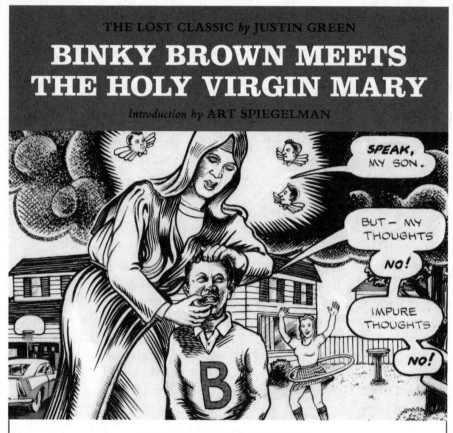

HIGH AND DRY

Richard Russo

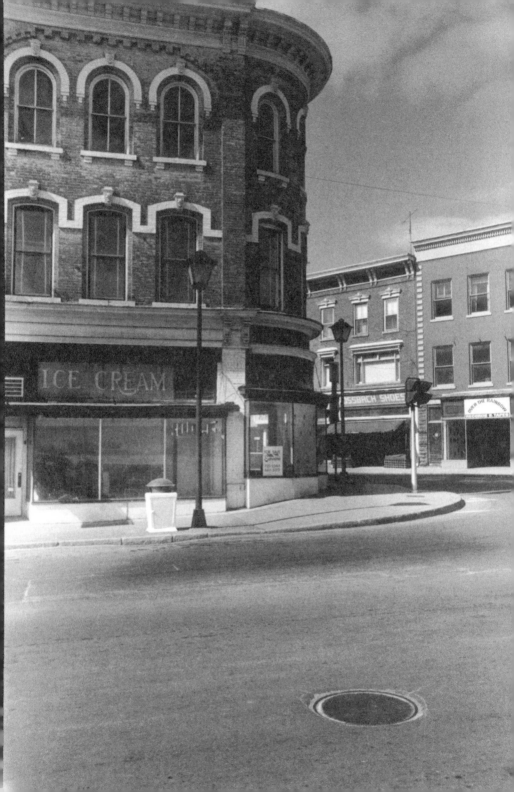

Pedrick's

A few years ago a friend of mine, passing the sign on the New York State Thruway for THE CENTRAL LEATHERSTOCKING REGION, misread the word *leatherstocking* for *laughingstock*, and thought, 'That must be where Russo's from.' She was right. I'm from Gloversville, just a few miles north in the foothills of the Adirondacks, a place that's easy to joke about unless you live there, as some of my family still do.

In its heyday nine out of ten dress gloves manufactured in the United States came from Gloversville. By the end of the nineteenth century craftsmen from all over Europe had flocked in, and for decades the gloves produced there were on a par with the finest made anywhere in the world. Back then glove cutting was governed by a guild. You apprenticed, as my maternal grandfather did, typically for two or three years. The primary tools of a guild-trained glove cutter's trade were his eye, his experience of animal skins and his imagination. It was my grandfather who gave me my very first lessons in art – though I doubt he would've put it like that – when he explained the challenge of making something truly fine and beautiful from an imperfect animal hide. After they're tanned, but before they go to the cutter, skins are rolled and brushed and finished to ensure smooth uniformity, but inevitably they retain some of nature's flaws. The true craftsman, he gave me to understand, works around these flaws or figures out how to incorporate them into the glove's natural folds or stitching. Each skin posed a problem whose solution required imagination. The glove cutter's job wasn't just to get as many gloves as possible out of a skin but to do so while minimizing its flaws.

Leather had been tanned in Fulton County, using the bark from local hemlock trees, since before the American Revolution.

Gloversville and neighbouring Johnstown were home to all things leather – shoes and coats and handbags and furniture, not only gloves. My other grandfather, who lived in an Italian village near Rome, had heard about this place where so many leather artisans had gathered in upstate New York, and so he journeyed to America in hope of making a living there as a shoemaker. From New York City he took the train north to Albany, then west as far as the Barge Canal hamlet of Fonda, where he followed the freight tracks north as far as Johnstown, where I was born years later. Did he have any real idea of where he was headed, or what his new life would be like? You tell me. Among the few material possessions he brought with him from the old country was an opera cape.

Both men had wretched timing. My Italian grandfather learned quickly that Fulton County wasn't New York City, and that few men in his new home would buy expensive custom-made shoes instead of comparatively inexpensive machine-made ones, so he had little choice but to become a shoe repairman. And by the time my maternal grandfather arrived in Gloversville from Vermont, the real craft of glove cutting was already under assault. By the end of World War I, many gloves were being 'pattern-cut'. (For a size 6 glove a size 6 pattern was affixed to the skin and cut around with shears.) Once he returned from World War II the process was largely mechanized by 'clicker' cutting machines that quickly stamped out pre-sized gloves, requiring the operator only to position the tanned skin under the machine's lethal blades and pull down on its mechanical arm. I was born in 1949, and by then there wasn't much demand for expensive handmade gloves or shoes, but both my grandfathers had made their big moves to Fulton County and staked their dubious claims, so there they remained. It was also during the first half of the twentieth century that chrome tanning, a chemical process that made leather more supple and water-resistant, and dramatically sped up the tanning process, became the industry standard, replacing traditional vegetable tanning and making tanneries even more hazardous, not just for the workers, but also for those who lived nearby and, especially, downstream. Speed, efficiency and technology had trumped art and craft.

That said, between 1890 and 1950 people in Gloversville made money, some of them a lot of it. Drive along Kingsboro Avenue, which parallels Main Street, and have a gander at the fine old houses set back from the street and well apart from one another, and you'll get a sense of the prosperity that at least some enjoyed until World War II. Even downtown Gloversville, which by the 1970s had become a Dresden-like ruin, still shows signs of that old wealth. The Andrew Carnegie Gloversville Free Library is as lovely as can be, and the old high school, which sits atop a gentle hill, bespeaks a community that once believed in itself and that good times would not be fleeting. On its sloping lawn stands a statue of Nathan Littauer, one of the richest men in the county, whose extended arm appears to point at the grand marble edifice of the Eccentric Club, which refused him membership because he was a Jew. Down the street is the recently restored Glove Theater, where I spent just about every Saturday afternoon of my adolescence. There was also a charming old hotel, the Kingsboro, in whose elegant dining room Monsignor Kreugler, whom I'd served as an altar boy at Sacred Heart Church, held weekly court after his last Sunday Mass. Since it was razed, visitors to Gloversville have had to stay in nearby Johnstown, out on the arterial highway that was supposed to breathe new life into the town but instead, all too predictably, allowed people to race by, without stopping or even slowing down, en route to Saratoga, Lake George or Montreal.

How quickly it all happened. In the fifties, on a Saturday afternoon, downtown Gloversville would be gridlocked with cars honking hellos at pedestrians. The sidewalks were so jammed with shoppers that, as a boy trapped among taller adults, I had to depend on my mother, herself no giant, to navigate us from one store to the next or, more harrowingly, across Main Street. Often, when we finished what we called our weekly 'errands', my mother and I would stop in at Pedrick's. Located next to City Hall, it was a dark, cool place, the only establishment of my youth that was air-conditioned, a long, thin wall whose service window allowed sodas and cocktails to be passed from the often raucous bar into the more respectable restaurant. Back then Pedrick's was always mobbed, even in the middle of a Saturday afternoon. Mounted on the wall of each booth was a mini jukebox whose movable mechanical pages were full of song listings. Selections made here – five for a quarter, if memory serves – were played on the real jukebox on the far wall. We always played the jukebox, a whole quarter's worth, while nursing sodas served so cold they made my teeth hurt. Sometimes, though, the music was drowned out by rowdy male laughter from the bar, where the wall-mounted television was tuned to a Yankees ball game, and if anybody hit a home run everyone in the restaurant knew it immediately. I remember listening intently to all the men's voices, trying to pick out my father's. He and my mother had separated when I was little, but he was still around town and I always imagined him on the other side of that wall in Pedrick's.

I also suspected that my mother, if she hadn't been saddled with me, would have preferred to be over there. She liked men, liked being among them, and the restaurant side was mostly women and kids and older people. Though I couldn't have put it into words, I had the distinct impression that the wall separating respectability from fun was very thin indeed. There was another jukebox in the bar, and sometimes it got cranked up loud enough to compete with whatever was playing on ours, and then my mother would say it was time to go, as if she feared the wall itself might come crashing down. To her, music getting pumped up like that could only mean one thing: that people over there were dancing, middle of the afternoon or not, and if she'd been there, it would have been her as well. A good decade after the end of World War II, Gloversville was still in a party mode, and regular Saturday festivities routinely continued right up to last call and often beyond, the town's prosperous citizens dancing and drinking at the Eccentric Club, the more middle-class folk in the blue-collar taverns along upper Main Street or, in summer, at the pavilion at nearby Caroga Lake, the poor (often the most recent immigrants with the lowest-paying tannery jobs) in the gin mills bordering South Main in the section of town referred to as the Gut, where arrests for drunkenness or indecency or belligerence were much more likely to be recorded in the local newspaper on Monday than comparable exploits at the Eccentric Club.

By the time I graduated from high school in 1967, you could have strafed Main Street with automatic weapon fire without endangering a soul. On Saturday afternoons the sidewalks were deserted, people in newly reduced circumstances shopping for bargains at the cheap, off-brand stores that had sprung up along the arterial. Jobless men would emerge from the pool hall or one of the seedy gin mills that sold cheap draught beer and rotgut rye, blinking into the afternoon light and flexing at the knees. Lighting up a smoke, they'd peer up Main Street in one direction, then down the other, as if wondering where the hell everybody went. By then the restaurant side of Pedrick's had closed, but since I turned eighteen that summer, now of legal drinking age, the other side was no longer off-limits. Now, though, it was quiet as a library, the half-dozen grizzled, solitary drinkers rotating on their stools when the door opened, as if out of the brightness the past might saunter in, trailing ten-dollar bills in its wake. Most of my friends were going to college close to home, at the Albany branch of the state university, or one of the small Catholic colleges, or the community college just down the road, whereas I was heading west to the University of Arizona in an old, dangerously underpowered Ford Galaxie and pulling a U-Haul that contained all my mother's worldly goods. She'd found a job, she told me, in nearby Phoenix, and she meant to escape once and for all this self-satisfied podunk town that everybody finally conceded had no future. Still, every now and then that summer of '67, I'd poke my head into Pedrick's to see if my father was among those drinking Utica Club draughts at the bar. But, like time itself, he too had moved on.

Globalism: A Primer

What happened? Lots of things. After World War II, about the same time men stopped wearing hats, women stopped wearing gloves. When Jackie Kennedy wore a pair at her husband's inauguration, the clock got turned back for a while, but the trend proved irreversible. More importantly, glove-making started going overseas where labour was cheap. Gloversville went bust the way Mike Campbell declares his bankruptcy in Hemingway's *The Sun Also Rises*, 'gradually and then suddenly'. The 'giant sucking sound' of globalism came to Gloversville decades early and with a vengeance. My maternal grandfather, who, despite being a veteran of two world wars, had been branded a Communist from the pulpit of Sacred Heart Church for being a union man, saw it coming even before crappy Asian-made gloves showed up in the shops, where a few buttons could be sewn on and the gloves stamped 'made in Gloversville'. Around Thanksgiving, the slow season in the glove business, workers in the skin mills got laid off, and every year it took a little longer for them to be called back. Worse, they weren't all rehired at once, which practice allowed the shop owners to remind their employees that things were different now. What mattered was moving inventory down the line, not quality. After all, Asians and Indians were doing what Gloversville men did at a quarter of the cost.

My grandfather, who came home from the Pacific with malaria and soon afterwards developed emphysema, was by then too sick to fight. He continued to work as always, refusing to cut corners and, as a result, making considerably less money than men who were willing to do things slapdash. The bosses could exploit him, give him the most flawed skins and treat him like a robot instead of the craftsman he was, but he claimed the one thing they couldn't order him to do was a bad job. But of course they didn't need to. You only had to look at how his narrow, concave chest heaved as he struggled to draw oxygen into his failing lungs to know he wouldn't be anybody's problem much longer. His wife, who'd survived the Depression, foresaw a diminished future. She began stocking the pantry with cans of wax beans and tuna fish earlier every year, aware that this time the lay offs would likely last longer, that her husband, who was growing sicker by the day, would be among the last called back. Jesus on his best day could do no more with loaves and fishes than my grandmother did with a pound of bacon. Still, it was just a matter of time.

Flight

So when I resolved to head out west to college, my mother decided to make it a jailbreak and come along, though for a long time she kept that plan to herself. You could hardly blame her for wanting out. By then she was divorced and still relatively young. We'd lived all those years in a well-maintained middle-class neighbourhood, sharing a modest two-family house, her parents in the two-bedroom, single-bath downstairs flat, she and I in the identically configured one above. My grandfather, who'd never before purchased anything he couldn't pay for with cash out of his wallet, bought that house on Helwig Street, I suspect, because he knew my parents' marriage was on the rocks and that my mother and I would need a place to live. Though she never would have admitted it, even to herself, she must have felt at least a little guilty about leaving now, fifteen years later, especially given her father's poor health. You don't get better from emphysema, you get worse, and his working days by then were done. An oxygen tank sat behind his chair in the living room. On cold days he couldn't go outdoors without a cloth mask, and even the easy stroll down to the mailbox at the end of the block tuckered him out. My mother kept her secret as long as she could, but eventually had to come clean. Having subsidized us over the years in small and sometimes larger ways, my grandparents were of the opinion that she couldn't make it out west on her own (she didn't own a car or even know how to drive), which made her even more determined to prove them wrong. In the months before we departed, they argued non-stop, and by the time we packed the U-Haul with what little my mother hadn't sold, they were barely speaking. Though aware of the discord, I was spared its worst effects because from the time I was little they had agreed never to argue in front of me; so I don't know what specific charges were levelled, who accused whom of what, how specific my grandparents were about their daughter's long history of underestimating life's costs and difficulties. Oddly enough, my sense was that their ongoing argument centred on Gloversville.

OK, maybe not the town itself. After all, my mother had grown up there and occasionally still harboured deep affection for it, an affection that would well up from some remote corner of her heart whenever she left. During her time in Phoenix she came to speak of Gloversville with something like longing, as if she'd been banished by cruel decree. Though I'd never encountered this before, the pattern was all too familiar to my grandparents. As a girl my mother couldn't wait to go away to college, but was terribly homesick when she got there and quit after a year, returning home to work as a telephone operator. Two short years later, when the army stationed my father in Georgia, she followed him there eagerly, like a bird released from a cage, but she didn't like the South and as soon as he shipped overseas she returned to Gloversville just as eagerly.

Once I came along, Gloversville had come to represent to my mother everything that was keeping her from living the finer life to which she was intended. She thought of herself as modern and freethinking, whereas her home town was backward and parochial. More than anything, what she longed for, first as a girl and later as a woman, was independence from scrutiny and interference, and the freedom to exercise her own judgement, which she believed to be excellent. All Gloversville offered was structure: church; neighbours; work; Sunday picnics with family at the lake – with her parents, right downstairs, second-guessing her every decision. If she stayed put, my grandparents argued, she'd be safe. But she didn't want to be safe. She wanted to be free.

Had I been asked my opinion, I might have weighed in, but probably not. As a high-school senior I was by definition already gone, as anxious as any other seventeen-year-old to embrace whatever came next. Like most of my friends, I knew that wouldn't be in Gloversville. For decades the mill owners had in effect run the town, and even as the leather industry slipped deeper into decline it kept other industries out, or so it was widely believed. If you were young, the conventional wisdom held that you had to go away and make something of yourself elsewhere – as a doctor or lawyer or pharmacist – before it made sense to return. My grandparents, unlike my mother, didn't hate Gloversville, but they understood the skin mills were finished, and anyway, mill life was a drudgery they wouldn't have wished on me even if it were lucrative. My grandfather, too young for the First World War and too old for the Second, had nevertheless served in both, and as a boy I assumed this was because he was very brave, very patriotic. Which he was, but war also offered him a respite from the shops. His wife, thinking of him on a ship in the South Pacific during World War II, was envious, if you can believe it, of the great adventure he was on, while she was left behind to measure out the long, grey days with their two daughters as best she could in a town she'd never wanted to move to anyway, because it took her away from her sisters. But neither she nor my grandfather blamed Gloversville for their circumscribed lives. They didn't spend a lot of time worrying about whether it was better or worse than other places. It was simply where they were, where they would remain.

And my own feelings about Gloversville? As a boy I'd been happy as a clam there. Our block on Helwig Street was neighbourly, with a grocery store situated diagonally across the street. My mother's sister and her family lived around the corner on Sixth Avenue, which meant I grew up surrounded by cousins. In kindergarten and first grade, my grandmother walked me to school in the morning and was there to meet me in the afternoon, and in the summers we went for walks to a lovely little park a few blocks away. On weekends it was often my grandfather who'd take my hand and together we'd head downtown for a bag of 'peatles', his peculiar word for red-skinned peanuts, stopping on the way back to visit with neighbours on their porches. By the time I was old enough to get my first bike and explore beyond Helwig Street, I'd discovered the magic of baseball and so, wooden bat over my shoulder, mitt dangling from my handlebars, I disappeared with friends for whole mornings or afternoons or both. At my aunt's there was a basketball hoop up over the garage, and during the long winters my cousin Greg and I kept the driveway shovelled meticulously so we could shoot baskets, even when it was so cold the net froze and you couldn't dribble the ball. Come autumn I raked leaves, stealing this job from my grandfather, who loved to do it, though he didn't always have sufficient breath. Sometimes he'd start the job and I finished while he snuck a cigarette around back of the house where my grandmother couldn't see him. Summers I mowed lawns, and winters I shovelled sidewalks, jobs I continued straight through high school, even though by then I had other part-time, after-school employment. I fell in love with one local girl after another. Was something missing? Anything amiss?

Yet when the time came I fled. I didn't *leave*, as everyone else my age was doing. I fled, fled as if I'd committed a crime and the authorities were closing in, the window of escape closing fast. As if I feared or even loathed the place I knew and the people I loved.

The Foothills

One winter, when I was ten or eleven and had expressed some fondness for or appreciation of our lives, my mother's face clouded over and she announced, '*You* are going to see something of the world outside Gloversville.'

Vacation, she meant, and that summer we went, just the two of us, to Martha's Vineyard. The island wasn't nearly so famous then, and I don't know where she got the idea. Probably somebody from General Electric had gone there. Much of what my mother knew about the world outside of Gloversville derived from her eight-to-five weekday life in the Computer Room in Schenectady, loading and unloading large wheel-like tape drives on to a computer the size of a bus. It was probably less powerful than today's low-end laptops, but engineers and programmers came from all over the US and even Europe to crunch their numbers, and my mother trusted these men as much as any newsreel or oracle. At any rate, one deep winter day a Manila envelope chock-full of brochures for posh hotels and graceful inns arrived from the island's chamber of commerce. My mother pored over them as if she feared there'd be a quiz when we stepped off the ferry. The resort she settled on was near Menemsha on the more remote and sparsely populated side of the island. The main inn was large and rambling, with a huge porch and an elegant dining room with a westward view of the sound, the better to view the magnificent sunsets. Between the inn and the water was a large sloping lawn dotted with tiny cottages, and it was one of these that we rented. Instead of being cheek by jowl with other vacationers, my mother reasoned, *we'd* have privacy *and* be closer to the water, though even a ten-year-old boy could plainly see that the cottages were cheaper. The attraction of this particular resort was that it operated on the American Plan, which meant that three meals a day were included; she could pay up front with no fear of surprise charges. She called twice that spring after we'd booked our stay, just to make sure she hadn't misunderstood that part.

Perhaps because my mother was so focused on how much it was going to cost, she didn't tumble to the fact that it was a Jewish resort, probably the only one on the island. Still, if her goal was to introduce me to something of the wider world, she'd chosen the right spot. Among our fellow vacationers were a dancer and a pianist and a playwright. Perhaps because of how out of place we appeared, we were immediately befriended. A young college student gave me tennis lessons when I showed up at the courts, no doubt looking forlorn, just as he and his girlfriend were finishing a match. When it rained one day, another couple took us into Oak Bluffs to see the gingerbread cottages. A woman roughly my mother's age, and also separated from her husband, sometimes came with us to the beach. She wore a startlingly brief swimsuit, which caused me to fall in love with her, and I remember being devastated when, instead of joining us in the dining room she went out on dinner dates to Edgartown and Vineyard Haven. Judging by the number of men who stopped by our table to introduce themselves, my mother, but for me, would have done the same.

Lest I miss the significance of all we observed that week, my mother provided a running commentary, as if she didn't trust me to arrive at valid conclusions. Notice, she said, how these people had manners, how they didn't dress or talk or shamble around like Gloversville folk. They were educated, as one day I would be, and to them home was New York or Boston, which somehow meant that they could stay for all of July, maybe even the whole summer, whereas because of *our* home, we had to scrimp and save for just one week. Notice, she said, how when people asked us where we were from and I said Gloversville, we then had to explain where it was, which meant our town wasn't the centre of anyone's universe but our own. 'But the Adirondacks are so beautiful,' people objected, anxious to concede that we lived someplace nice. 'The *foothills* of the Adirondacks,' my mother clarified, giving me to understand that we, neither up nor down, had cleverly contrived to have the worst of both worlds.

It was an expensive week in more ways than one. My mother had financed the trip by brown-bagging an entire year's worth of cheese sandwiches instead of going out for lunch with her co-workers, and we'd blown the whole wad in seven short days, after which there was nothing to do but return to our foothills. The island ferry dropped us in Wood's Hole, where we waited for a bus to take us to Providence, then for another to Albany, and finally for the one to the Four Corners in Gloversville. By the time we arrived we were so tapped out that my mother had to borrow money from my grandparents until she could collect her next pay cheque at GE. Even more discouraging, from her perspective, was that nobody wanted to hear about the marvellous island we'd visited, the classy people we'd met, the exciting things we'd done. No one expressed the slightest desire to duplicate our experience the following summer, though my mother was anxious to share the brochures she'd saved, the ferry schedule, the postcards she purchased as mementos. I managed to make matters worse, as I usually did back then, by telling her how glad I was to be home. What I meant, of course, was that I'd missed my grandparents and my cousins and not one but two American Legion baseball games. What she heard, though, was that I preferred the place she loathed. For a whole year she'd sacrificed to show me something better, and I had failed to appreciate it.

All right, then, she decided, no more *showing*. From then on she meant to lay down the law. 'You're *going* to college,' she informed me, as if by saying I was glad to be home, I'd called into question that long-range goal. 'You're getting *out* of this place. Do you understand?' When I said I did, she asked me the same question again, and only when I gave the same answer did she go to the store and buy more sliced American cheese and rye bread. These future savings would now go into my college fund. By the time we left for Arizona they amounted to a little over $4,000. Not much, unless you think of it as eight years' worth of cheese sandwiches in 1960s dollars.

But if she thought I wasn't paying attention on Martha's Vineyard, she was wrong. I'd been as enchanted as she was by the island and everyone we'd met there. I'd loved the crashing waves and clam chowder and tennis so much that I returned home feeling ashamed of where we lived, of our neighbours whose leaves I raked and snow I shovelled and lawns I mowed, and of how people further down Helwig Street sat shirtless on their sloping porches in warm weather, scratching their bellies and leaning forward when a car they didn't recognize rounded the corner, wondering out loud who *that* was and where they were headed. After Martha's Vineyard I noticed things about our family, too: the way we talked over one another at holiday gatherings, our voices rising, screeching *No, no, you're telling it wrong*, because, of course, these stories belonged to all of us and we knew their details by heart. Martha's Vineyard people didn't interrupt; before entering the conversation they waited politely until whoever was speaking had finished. 'There's no reason to raise your voice here,' my mother had to keep reminding me. When we saw people in the dining room we'd met the day before, everybody stood up and we all shook hands. 'Did you notice how clean his fingernails were?' my mother whispered when whoever it was had left, and I knew I was supposed to compare them to the fingernails of men who worked in the skin mills.

What I'd noticed, actually, was that none of the men on the island were missing fingers. As tanning and glove-making became increasingly mechanized, there were more and more accidents, more men maimed. To make them less cumbersome and unwieldy, the skins were halved, and cowhides in particular were too thick for gloves, which meant they had to be split. The staking machines used to stretch the skins, yielding more square footage, were particularly lethal, as were the embossing machines that used giant plates to give the leather a nice grain, and these descended with a force of 1,000 pounds per square inch. And of course the clicker-cutter operators had to make sure their fingers were outside the perimeter of the machines when the skins were stamped. Every stage of the process now required machines and the hides were fed into these by hand, the very hand you'd lose if your mind wandered for an instant.

Blades sharp enough to sever a tanned skin were fitted with safety devices whose ostensible purpose was to keep them from lopping off fingers, but of course their real purpose was to protect the mill's owner from lawsuits. Because if you work the line, you're paid by the cubic foot of skin you process, and if you've got kids to feed and clothe, the very first thing you'll do is disable the safety mechanism that slows down your output. This is understood by everyone, including the foreman who turns his back while you do it. It's also understood that sooner or later something will go wrong. Work this mind-numbingly repetitive invites daydreaming, and your own safety often depends on people you're working with, because if you're pushing a skin into a machine, there's likely someone on the other side tugging it out. Eventually one of you will mess up. You'll slip or lunge and enter the machine with the same hand that people who summer on Martha's Vineyard shake with, after which your thumbnail will never be dirty again.

The Royal Society Beam House

Two years ago my daughter Kate was married in London at the Royal Society, a series of underground vaults, formerly wine cellars, just off the Strand and a few short blocks from Trafalgar Square. Our son-in-law, Tom, is English and the couple would be living in London, so there was no question of holding the ceremony in the States. The wedding was relatively small: Tom's family, some friends from the Slade Art School where they met, a few of Kate's college friends. Understandably, given the distance and expense, not many family members from our side of the Atlantic made the trip. The exception was my cousin Greg, with whom I shot wintry baskets when we were kids, and his wife, Carole, both of whom have lived their whole lives in Gloversville. 'Quite a ways from Helwig Street,' Greg said, taking in the venue. It wasn't as grand as 'Royal Society' might suggest, but the arching brick vaults, candlelit for the occasion, were impressive. There's nothing remotely like it in an upstate mill town. The person who would've appreciated it the most, who'd have seen it as vindication for all those cheese sandwiches, was my mother, but she'd died that summer after a long illness.

In any event, the how-far-we'd-all-come theme occupied the American contingent while we waited for the bride and groom to finish having their photos taken. Nat Sobel, my friend and literary agent, immediately took to my cousin, telling Greg that as a boy he, too, had lived near a tannery that released its toxins into the local stream, the water running a different colour each day depending on the dye batch. And so, flutes of Prosecco in hand, we began swapping stories about the worst jobs we'd ever had.

I recalled the summer of my non-union construction job in Johnstown. Most other summers I'd been able to get union work at an hourly rate nearly twice what men were making at the skin mills. That meant joining the labourers' union, of course, and my father had to pay my dues while I was away at college. That year, though, jobs were scarce and I hadn't got one. Non-union construction was a different world. The first week we had to drill holes in a concrete abutment, not a difficult task if you have a drill. We didn't. What we did have was a jackhammer and a foreman who was unconstrained by conventional thinking. The jackhammer guy and I formed a team that afternoon. Balancing his weapon on my shoulder, I held on for dear life as we jacked horizontally into the wall, sharp shards of concrete blasting back into our faces. Another thing we didn't have was a spare set of goggles.

This story will win a lot of 'bad job' storytelling contests unless your competitor has worked in the beam house of a skin mill doing the wettest, foulest, lowest-paid, and most dangerous jobs in the whole tannery. Greg had worked in one for a couple of months one summer, and his younger brother, Jim, for much longer. The first and probably nastiest job in the beaming operation was unloading the skins, which arrived at the loading dock on railroad cars still reeking from the slaughterhouses. The word 'skin' probably gives the wrong impression. Most people have never seen a hide – sheep, pig, calf, cow – unattached from its living owner. Stretched out flat they're big and, especially in the case of cows, surprisingly heavy. The top side is still covered with coarse hair, the underside with patches of maggot-infested flesh and gristle. The stench? You don't want to know, but imagine – if you can – what it must be like to spend an eight-hour shift unloading a railcar full of them in extreme temperatures.

Later, inside the beam house, things got even worse, the skins were submerged in huge vats and soaked for days in a chemical bath that stripped off most of the hair and the last of the clinging flesh. Naturally, these chemicals could easily do the same to hair on the hands and forearms of men hired to hoist the soaked skins out of the vats, so they were issued long rubber gloves. You'd think the skins would be lighter minus the hair and flesh, but you'd be wrong, because untanned skins reabsorb the moisture lost during transport and this cleansing. The soaking also turns the heavy skins slippery. The rubber gloves make the slick skins harder to grab hold of, as does the fact that you're bent over the vat and standing on a wet concrete floor.

At some point, like the men farther down the line who prod the tanned skins into staking machines and roller presses, you'll do what you know you shouldn't. *You will take off the rubber gloves,* because then the job is immediately easier. At the end of your shift you will wash your hands and arms vigorously with the coarsest soap you can find, and when you get home you'll do it again. You'll gradually lose the hair on your hands and forearms, but otherwise, for a while, everything seems fine. OK, sometimes your fingers itch. A little at first, then a lot. Your skin begins to feel odd, almost loose, as if moisture has somehow gotten beneath it and what you're trying to scratch isn't on the surface. Finally it itches so bad you can't stand it anymore, and you grab your thumb or forefinger and give the skin a twist, then a pull. The skin, several layers of it, comes away in one piece, like the finger of a latex glove. (On the other side of the Atlantic, at the Royal Society, my cousin demonstrates with his thumb, pulling off the imaginary prophylactic of skin, as everybody winces.) Instantly, the itching becomes stinging pain as the air impinges on your raw flesh. Later, someone will come around with a jar of black goop and you'll plunge your raw thumb into it, the coolness offering at least some relief, and for a while you go back to wearing the rubber gloves.

This is only the beginning though, just the beam house's way of saying hello when all you want to say is goodbye – to the skins, the foul chemical air, even your co-workers, because, let's face it, the ones who've been at it for a while, many of them with fifth-grade educations, aren't quite right. You all make the same shitty pay, but at the end of the summer you get to leave and for that the others hate you. Meanwhile, you can't imagine getting used to work like this, nor that the day will ever come when the lunch whistle sounds and instead of going outside into the fresh air you'll decide it's easier just to stay where you are, take a seat on a pallet of decomposing hides, wipe your hands on your pants and eat your sandwich right there – because what the hell, it's been for ever since you really smelled or tasted anything anyway. Plus, in the beam house there's entertainment. You can watch the rats chase the terrified cats that have been introduced to hunt them.

As my cousin relates this story, which I'm hearing for the first time, I become conscious of being in two places at once. I have one dry, wingtipped foot in the candlelit world of a fancy arts society in London in 2007; the other work-booted foot is sloshing through the wet, slippery beam-house floor in Gloversville, New York, circa 1970. That younger me isn't a novelist, or even a husband or father. He's just a twenty-year-old whose future can be stolen from him, who might indeed be complicit in the theft, because I remember all too well how sometimes, late in August, working road construction with my father, I'd think about not going back to college and maybe just staying on to do that hard, honest work he and his friends did all year round. The older me, now holding an empty champagne flute, feels guilty – and not, when I think of my home town, for the first time – to be where I am, like I've cheated destiny or, worse, swapped destinies with some other poor sod – to be where I am. My throat begins to constrict dangerously, though I can't tell if that's due to my cousin's story or because at this moment the wedding party returns – Kate absolutely radiant in the first hour of her marriage, and her sister Emily, who will marry the next year, laughing her throaty laugh and looping her arm through her fiancé's. Both smart, confident, beautiful young women, their feet planted squarely in the candlelit world before them, the only one that exists this day. The time might come when they too feel haunted, guilty about what they've been spared in life, keenly aware of how things, but for the grace of God, might have gone otherwise. But that day seems a long way off.

'More Prosecco?' one of the waitresses wants to know.

'Yes, please,' I tell her. 'Absolutely. Lay it on me. Right to the brim.'

Civic Integrity

Not long after Kate's wedding, a package with a Gloversville return address arrived at our home in Maine. It contained two books. The first was a copy of my novel *Bridge of Sighs*, which takes place in a fictional upstate New York town based on Gloversville, the story of two working-class boys, one who never leaves, the other who flees and never returns. The man who sent it in hope of an autograph was Vincent DeSantis, who had spent most of his life in Gloversville, as he explained in the accompanying letter, and identified strongly with my character Lucy Lynch, who'd done the same thing. Clearly he thought he was writing to the boy who'd got away, and I couldn't really blame him. Since the death of my grandparents and my father, I've returned to Gloversville less and less frequently. The other book in his package was *Toward Civic Integrity: Re-establishing the Micropolis*, written by, well, Vincent DeSantis, and seeing this my heart sank, as it always does when I get sent books I haven't asked for with a view toward my endorsement. But Mr DeSantis wasn't looking for a blurb and his book, despite its rather scholarly title, wasn't an esoteric work of non-fiction. It was about Gloversville, and the question he posed was whether it and other small cities had a future in the global twenty-first century or were in inevitable and irreversible decline. 'All is not lost in your home town,' the author assured me. 'A network of dedicated and talented individuals has lately been working to reassemble the pieces of this fractured micropolis.' My knee-jerk reaction to this Humpty-Dumpty sentiment was, *Yeah, right. All the king's horses and all the king's men.* Integrity indeed. I tossed the book on a tall stack of volumes whose common denominator was that I was unlikely to read them in this or any other lifetime. Not interested.

Yet that wasn't true, was it? After my mother's death, I'd been thinking a lot about her lifelong love–hate relationship with Gloversville. My cousin Greg had also been much on my mind. A few years earlier he'd had open-heart surgery to replace a malfunctioning valve, but he still couldn't sleep lying down and was getting by on a couple hours a night. Since London, I'd tried to keep in touch, though when I called to enquire about his health, he always gave me his standard line, 'Nah, I'm doing great for an old guy.' Then we'd talk about what our kids were up to and what movies we'd seen and whether I was working on something new. But eventually the talk would turn to Gloversville: who'd been jailed or diagnosed, who'd gone into a nursing home or died. When I mentioned I couldn't get his beam-house story out of my mind, he said, 'Oh, hell, that's nothing,' then launched into a litany of Gloversville woe I was all too familiar with. Men mangled by machines, men slowly poisoned, men killed in accidents. The three guys who worked the spray line in one mill all died of the same exotic testicular cancer, a case so outrageous it had made *The New York Times*. Not to mention the retarded boy hired to clean out the blues room, so named because the chrome used on these tanned skins turned them blue. The world of leather is full of scraps – strips of worthless skin and hoof and tail – and every now and then these had to be disposed of and the whole lethal place, including its giant vats, swamped out. One evening, when this kid didn't come home, his mother called the shop to see if he was still around. No, she was told, everybody from the day shift had left. The following morning he was found dead on the floor, asphyxiated by fumes. Another man, nearing retirement age, was working a press when his partner inadvertently stepped on the pedal that starts the rollers, catching the man's hand – more like a fin, now – in the mechanism. Another day, when it was weirdly cold on the floor, the foreman sent a man to fire up a boiler that hadn't been inspected in twenty years and it promptly blew up, killing him. Stories upon stories, each reminding my cousin of other men who died, their families uncompensated. Some dated back to my grandfather's days, stories I'd heard so many times that I know them as well as Greg does, but I understand why he needs to repeat them. The guys who lived this life in this world are, like World War II veterans, mostly gone. Somebody *should* give a shit.

For many months the vague boosterism of Vincent DeSantis's letter, together with my suspicion that his book was probably built on a shaky foundation of sentimentality and unguarded optimism, allowed me to let his book rest where I'd tossed it so contemptuously, until one day, suffering a rare attack of fair play (and perhaps just a little curious), I picked it up and started reading. To my surprise I discovered that DeSantis and I had quite a lot in common, sharing many political and cultural convictions. It's clear to both of us, for instance, that the old manufacturing jobs that provided the economic lifeblood of towns like Gloversville are gone for good, no matter how much we might wish otherwise. We also agree that an America that makes less *is* less. He's as profoundly interested as I am in the New Urban Movement and just as convinced that the time has come to start planning communities for people instead of their cars because the days of cheap energy are dwindling down to a precious few. A micropolis, as he defines it, is, like Gloversville, a small city of ten to fifty thousand inhabitants, and he argues persuasively that such communities might be well positioned to prosper in a less auto-centric future. They have the kind of infrastructure – a downtown – that will be essential, assuming urban renewal hadn't razed it back in the sixties. Ironically, abandoned mills, rather than being a blight on the landscape, could become part of the solution once they've been retrofitted to new purposes. Towns like Gloversville once had a rationale of their own, which is more than can be said for any suburb, and while their new incarnation is unlikely to have much in common with the old one, that doesn't mean it won't be just as valid. What Mr DeSantis and I see eye to eye on, strangely enough, is the future, or at least a *possible* future.

But what a nest of thorns the past can be. 'The glove industry sustained Gloversville in fine style,' he enthuses. 'Factories were full of glove-cutters and glove-makers, and the sound of sewing machines and the smell of finished leather . . . were a part of everyday life in Gloversville.' I, too, happen to love the smell of finished leather, but I can smell it only because I never worked in a beam house; and while I could be wrong, I'll hazard a wild guess that Mr DeSantis never did either. But weren't there women in his family, as there were in mine, who sewed gloves for close to fifty years and when they finally retired earned pensions of less than fifty dollars a month? Mr DeSantis's view of the Gloversville of our youth – it turns out he's just a year older than I – isn't false but it rests on a foundation of carefully selected facts and memories. For him, the old days when the skin mills were in full swing were good because of the wealth and prosperity they created. He remembers his aunts and uncles lamenting the loss of jobs overseas, but generously concludes that 'in fairness to the glove companies . . . failure to take advantage . . . of cheap labour would have been tantamount to corporate suicide'. Well, OK, OK, but if a dramatic phrase like 'corporate suicide' fairly describes the tanneries' untenable options in 1950, by the same token shouldn't disregard for the health and welfare of the workers who created their fortunes qualify as 'corporate murder'? Or, coupled with a bottom-line mentality that led so many to flee the scene of the crime, 'corporate rape'? Chrome tanning was never anything but lethal, its by-products including lime, chlorine, formaldehyde, sulphuric acid, chromium III, glycol ether EB, Toluene, Xylol, magnesium sulphate, lead, copper and zinc, to name just a few. Anyone who believes that tanneries didn't know they were releasing carcinogens into the air, water and landfills, probably also assumes that cigarette companies had no idea their product might be hazardous to the health of smokers. In addition to chasing cheap labour overseas, the big glove shops were fleeing – successfully for the most part – their own day of reckoning. New environmental restrictions imposed by the Department of Labor and later by the Occupational Safety and Health Administration were making the industry unprofitable, whereas on the other side of the world there were no such restrictions (and wouldn't be for decades). When it became clear that the tanneries wouldn't be allowed to continue dumping their waste in the stream, they left rather than pay the sewer taxes levied to support the new facility specifically designed and built to dispose of their waste more safely. Off they blithely went to pollute the Ganges and the Philippines, leaving behind a veritable Love Canal of carcinogens, the clean-up bill to be paid by the poisoned.

Of course Gloversville in its heyday, as Mr DeSantis rightly points out, was more than glove shops and tanneries. A community, even one dominated by a single industry that hates competition, still needs grocery stores, bakeries, restaurants, insurance agencies, clothing stores and car dealerships. Residents need schools and teachers and libraries and a movie theatre, and when you lose the industry that underlies these other enterprises, these inevitably become endangered. It's not just the mills that are abandoned when the good times – if that's what they were – stop rolling. You also lose, as Mr DeSantis points out, part of your identity, your reason for being, a shared sense of purpose that's hard to quantify. People who make things are often proud of what they make, especially if it endures. One summer my father and I worked on Exit 23 on the New York State Thruway, and thereafter were never able to get on that cloverleaf without sharing a knowing look. But sometimes people are so proud of what they make that they willingly overlook its true cost. That Gloversville once had an identity based on a common sense of purpose is a potent argument. It is used, for instance, to explain the construction of the great cathedrals of Europe, and what are they if not symbols of communal wealth and belief? Given the technology of the day, the pyramids are even more awe-inspiring, at least until one remembers they were built with slave labour. Closer to home, the Confederacy was a case study in shared values and cultural identity, whose foundation, of course, was slavery; not long after the war that freed its victims, Margaret Mitchell invited the nation to lament the passing of those halcyon days that were now gone with the wind, and a great many still do.

Do I sound bitter?

High and Dry

A better question might be whether such bitterness can be justified. The optimism of Vincent DeSantis, in both his letter and his book, clearly struck a chord, and my reaction to it begs several questions. Among them: is it possible I don't *want* Humpty-Dumpty to be put back together again? Is Gloversville's current 'shattered state' what I think, deep down, it somehow deserves? When I listen to my cousin's stories about men diagnosed, men maimed, men poisoned, men killed, isn't part of what I feel a grim satisfaction that so little in fact has changed? Moreover, if it's bitterness I'm feeling toward my home town, is it even my own, born of my own experience, or my mother's, a second-hand resentment I internalized as a kid and, as such, unrelated to stories of the beam house, the spray line, the tanning room? Perhaps, most important, are all the old stories of injury and disease and death really just proxies, a chance for my cousin and me to vent rage that as boys we were too young to understand? After all, we witnessed the slow but fatal strangulation of our own grandfather, a man we both loved. Are we still, all these years later, bent on assigning blame?

Leather was a vertical industry. It went from low and wet in the beam house to high and dry in the sewing and cutting rooms, where the work was slightly better paid and less dangerous. I remember standing on the sidewalk below and sighting along my mother's index finger up to the top floor of the glove shop where my grandfather worked, and sensing her pride in him. I think I understood the law of verticality even then. But appearances were deceiving, and though he was as yet undiagnosed, my grandfather's luck had already run out. Machines and the relentless drumbeat of piecework, together with a shorter work season, guaranteed that he'd die a poor man. And while the tanned skins were dry by the time they got to the top floor, they were also full of hide dust that, breathed over a lifetime, was toxic. For years my grandfather didn't worry about his shortness of breath. He'd come home from the Pacific with malaria, and maybe that explained it. In the early sixties, when it became impossible to ignore his worsening symptoms, he was finally diagnosed with emphysema by doctors who had little doubt that his occupation was a contributing factor. But he was also an occasional smoker, and never stopped, not entirely, even when he knew that each cigarette reduced the time he had left. I doubt he would've sued his employers even if he thought he could win because, as he would have been the first to point out, the glove shops had put bread on his family's table for all those years, and what would he have done, how would he otherwise have made a living? Bitterness and recrimination weren't worth the little breath he still had. In his way my grandfather was a philosopher, and he would've wanted me to be suspicious of any bitterness I harboured on his behalf, just as he would've reminded me of the terrible possibility that what nourishes us in this life may in some instances be the very thing that steals it from us.

When you take all this into account, it might be fair to ask why I, of all people, should continue to take his death and the betrayal of countless others so personally. After all, I never spent a minute in the beam house. Unlike my cousins, on hot summer days I don't have to lance with a needle the hard pustules that still form on their hands thirty years after the fact. What right does one who'd fled at the earliest opportunity have to speak for those who remained behind? I'm not, I like to think, an unforgiving man. Then why, when Vincent DeSantis informs me that all is not lost in my home town, does rage roil up uninvited out of the depths? Wouldn't it be better to make the peace my mother never made? When the end drew near, she asked that her ashes be scattered not in Gloversville but on Martha's Vineyard, where she'd spent a week of her life. She knew that I vacationed there with my family every year. Maybe it wasn't her home, but home wasn't her home either. My cousin Greg, on the other hand, knows where home is. He has one and he lives there. When he tells me stories about men diagnosed, men maimed, men poisoned, men killed, it's his home he's talking about.

I'm often asked why I so seldom return to Gloversville, where I'm told people are proud of my success. I've written too many lies about the place, I like to explain, which is true enough. Reality chafes imagination and vice versa. And is there any need for me to return when, in a sense, I've never really left? Read my novels, even the ones not set in upstate New York, and you'll see Fulton County reflected on just about every page. It drove my mother crazy. She'd been hoping for a clean getaway, and mine was anything but. All too often my decisions in the present are linked to my Gloversville past. For instance. Because coastal Maine, where my wife and I live, is remote and I now have to travel a good deal, we recently got an apartment in downtown Boston with easy access to the airport and train station. We looked in a lot of different areas but finally settled, as I knew we would, in the Leather District, a neighbourhood of mostly abandoned leather businesses. We're on the seventh floor of an eight-storey building, high and dry, which I think would have made my grandfather smile. One night shortly after we moved in, my wife was away and I found myself navigating through the unfamiliar television channels, stopping on one called American Life, which was playing an episode of *77 Sunset Strip*, which was followed by *Bourbon Street Beat* and *Surfside 6*, all shows we watched when I was a boy stretched out on my grandparents' living-room floor on Helwig Street. At some point I became aware of the tears streaming down my face, aware that I wasn't in Boston anymore, not really, but rather back in Gloversville, the only place I've ever called home and meant by that what people mean who never leave. ∎

THE FARM

Mark Twain

My uncle, John A. Quarles, was a farmer, and his place was in the country four miles from Florida. He had eight children, and fifteen or twenty negroes, and was also fortunate in other ways. Particularly in his character. I have not come across a better man than he was. I was his guest for two or thee months every year, from the fourth year after we removed to Hannibal till I was eleven or twelve years old. I have never consciously used him or his wife in a book, but his farm has come very handy to me in literature, once or twice. In 'Huck Finn' and in 'Tom Sawyer Detective' I moved it down to Arkansas. It was all of six hundred miles, but it was no trouble, it was not a very large farm; five hundred acres, perhaps, but I could have done it if it had been twice as large. And as for the morality of it, I cared nothing for that; I would move a State if the exigencies of literature required it.

It was a heavenly place for a boy, that farm of my Uncle John's. The house was a double log one, with a spacious floor (roofed in) connecting it with the kitchen. In the summer the table was set in the middle of that shady and breezy floor, and the sumptuous meals – well, it makes me cry to think of them. Fried chicken; roast pig; wild and tame turkeys, ducks, and geese; venison just killed; squirrels, rabbits, pheasants, partridges, prairie chickens; home-made bacon and ham; hot biscuits, hot batter-cakes, hot buckwheat cakes, hot 'wheatbread', hot rolls, hot corn pone; fresh corn boiled on the ear, succotash, butter-beans, string beans, tomatoes, peas, Irish potatoes, sweet potatoes; buttermilk, sweet milk, 'clabber'; watermelons, musk melons, canteloups – all fresh from the garden – apple pie, peach pie, pumpkin pie, apple dumplings, peach cobbler – I can't remember the rest. The way that the things were cooked was perhaps the main splendor – particularly a certain few of the dishes. For instance, the corn bread, the hot biscuits and wheatbread, and the fried chicken. These things have never been properly cooked in the North – in fact, no one there is able to learn the art, so far as my experience goes. The North thinks it knows how to make corn bread, but this is gross superstition. Perhaps no bread in the world is quite as good as Southern corn bread, and perhaps no bread in the world is quite so bad as the Northern imitation of it. The North seldom tries to fry chicken, and this is well; the art cannot be learned north of the line of Mason and Dixon, nor anywhere in Europe. This is not hearsay; it is experience that is speaking. In Europe it is imagined that the custom of serving various kinds of bread blazing hot is 'American', but that is too broad a spread: it is custom in the South, but is much less than that in the North. In the North and in Europe hot bread is considered unhealthy. This is probably another fussy superstition, like the European superstition that ice-water is unhealthy. Europe does not need ice-water, and does not drink it; and yet, notwithstanding this, its word for it is better than ours, because it describes it, whereas ours doesn't. Europe calls it 'iced' water. Our word describes water made from melted ice – a drink which has a characterless taste, and which we have but little acquaintance with.

It seems a pity that the world should throw away so many good things merely because they are unwholesome. I doubt if God has given us any refreshment which, taken in moderation, is unwholesome, except microbes. Yet there are people who strictly deprive themselves of each and every eatable, drinkable and smokable which has in any way acquired a shady reputation. They pay this price for health. And health is all they get for it. How strange it is; it is like paying out your whole fortune for a cow that has gone dry.

The farm-house stood in the middle of a very large yard, and the yard was fenced on three sides with rails and on the rear side with high palings; against these stood the smoke-house; beyond the palings was the orchard, beyond the orchard were the negro quarter and the tobacco fields. The front yard was entered over a stile, made of sawed-off logs of graduated heights; I do not remember any gate.

In a corner of the front yard were a dozen lofty hickory trees and a dozen black walnuts, and in the nutting season riches were to be gathered there.

Down a piece, abreast the house, stood a little log cabin against the rail fence; and there the woody hill fell sharply away, past the barns, the corn-crib, the stables and the tobacco-curing house, to a limpid brook which sang along over its gravelly bed and curved and frisked in and out and here and there and yonder in the deep shade of overhanging foliage and vines – a divine place for wading, and it had swimming-pools, too, which were forbidden to us and therefore much frequented by us. For we were little Christian children, and had early been taught the value of forbidden fruit.

In the little log cabin lived a bedridden white-headed slave woman whom we visited daily, and looked upon with awe, for we believed she was upwards of a thousand years old and had talked with Moses. The younger negroes credited these statistics, and had furnished them to us in good faith. We accommodated all the details which came to us about her; and so we believed that she had lost her health in the long desert-trip coming out of Egypt, and had never been able to get it back again. She had a round bald place on the crown of her head, and we used to creep around and gaze at it in reverent silence, and reflect that it was caused by fright through seeing Pharaoh drowned. We called her 'Aunt' Hannah, Southern fashion. She was superstitious like the other negroes; also, like them, she was deeply religious. Like them, she had great faith in prayer, and employed it in all ordinary exigencies, but not in cases where a dead certainty of result was urgent. Whenever witches were around she tied up the remnant of her wool in little tufts, with white thread, and this promptly made the witches impotent.

All the negroes were friends of ours, and with those of our own age we were in effect comrades. I say in effect, using the phrase as a modification. We were comrades, and yet not comrades; color and condition interposed a subtle line which both parties were conscious of, and which rendered complete fusion impossible. We had a faithful and affectionate good friend, ally and adviser in 'Uncle Dan'l', a middle-aged slave whose head was the best one in the negro-quarter, whose sympathies were wide and warm, and whose heart was honest and simple and knew no guile. He has served me well, these many, many years. I have not seen him for more than half a century, and yet spiritually I have had his welcome company a good part of that time, and have staged him in books under his own name and as 'Jim', and carted him all around – to Hannibal, down the Mississippi on a raft, and even across the Desert of Sahara in a balloon – and he has endured it all with the patience and friendliness and loyalty which were his birthright. It was on the farm that I got my strong liking for his race and my appreciation of certain of its fine qualities. This feeling and this estimate have stood the test of sixty years and more and have suffered no impairment. The black face is as welcome to me now as it was then.

In my schoolboy days I had no aversion to slavery. I was not aware that there was anything wrong about it. No one arraigned it in my hearing; the local papers said nothing against it; the local pulpit taught us that God approved it, that it was a holy thing, and that the doubter need only look in the Bible if he wished to settle his mind – and then the texts were read aloud to us to make the matter sure; if the slaves themselves had an aversion to slavery they were wise and said nothing. In Hannibal we seldom saw a slave misused; on the farm, never.

There was, however, one small incident of my boyhood days which touched this matter, and it must have meant a good deal to me or it would not have stayed in my memory, clear and sharp, vivid and shadowless, all these slow-drifting years. We had a little slave boy whom we had hired from some one, there in Hannibal. He was from the Eastern Shore of Maryland, and had been brought away from his family and his friends, half way across the American continent, and sold. He was a cheery spirit, innocent and gentle, and the noisiest creature that ever was, perhaps. All day long he was singing, whistling, yelling, whooping, laughing – it was maddening, devastating, unendurable. At last, one day, I lost all my temper, and went raging to my mother, and said Sandy had been singing for an hour without a single break, and I couldn't stand it, and *wouldn't* she please shut him up. The tears came into her eyes, and her lip trembled, and she said something like this –

'Poor thing, when he sings, it shows that he is not remembering, and that comforts me; but when he is still, I am afraid he is thinking, and I cannot bear it. He will never see his mother again; if he can sing, I must not hinder it, but be thankful for it. If you were older, you would understand me; then that friendless child's noise would make you glad.'

It was a simple speech, and made up of small words, but it went home, and Sandy's noise was not a trouble to me any more. She never used large words, but she had a natural gift for making small ones do effective work. She lived to reach the neighborhood of ninety years, and was capable with her tongue to the last – especially when a meanness or an injustice roused her spirit. She has come handy to me several times in my books, where she figures as Tom Sawyer's 'Aunt Polly'. I fitted her out with a dialect, and tried to think up other improvements for her, but did not find any. I used Sandy once, also; it was in 'Tom Sawyer'; I tried to get him to whitewash the fence, but it did not work. I do not remember what name I called him by in the book.

I can see the farm yet, with perfect clearness. I can see all its belongings, all its details: the family room of the house, with a 'trundle' bed in one corner and a spinning-wheel in another – a wheel whose rising and falling wail, heard from a distance, was the mournfulest of all sounds to me, and made me homesick and low-spirited, and filled my atmosphere with the wandering spirits of the dead; the vast fireplace, piled high, on winter nights, with flaming hickory logs from whose ends a sugary sap bubbled out but did not go to waste, for we scraped it off and ate it; the lazy cat spread out on the rough hearthstones, the drowsy dogs braced against the jambs and blinking; my aunt in one chimney corner knitting, my uncle in the other smoking his corn-cob pipe; the slick and carpetless oak floor faintly mirroring the dancing flame-tongues and freckled with black indentations where fire-coals had popped out and died a leisurely death; half a dozen children romping in the background twilight; 'split'-bottomed chairs here and there, some with rockers; a cradle – out of service, but waiting, with confidence; in the early cold mornings a snuggle of children, in shirts and chemises, occupying the hearthstone and procrastinating – they could not bear to leave that comfortable place and go out on the wind-swept floor-space between the house and the kitchen where the general tin basin stood, and wash.

Along outside of the front fence ran the country road; dusty in the summertime, and a good place for snakes – they liked to lie in it and sun themselves; when they were rattlesnakes or puff adders, we killed them; when they were black snakes, or racers, or belonged to the fabled 'hoop' breed, we fled, without shame; when they were 'house-snakes' or 'garters' we carried them home and put them in Aunt Patsy's work-basket for a surprise; for she was prejudiced against snakes, and always when she took the basket in her lap and they began to climb out of it it disordered her mind. She never could seem to get used to them; her opportunities went for nothing. And she was always cold towards bats, too, and could not bear them; and yet I think a bat is as friendly a bird as there is. My mother was Aunt Patsy's sister, and had the same wild superstitions. A bat is beautifully soft and silky; I do not know any creature that is pleasanter to the touch, or is more grateful for caressings, if offered in the right spirit. I know all about these coleoptera, because our great cave, three miles below Hannibal, was multitudinously stocked with them, and often I brought them home to amuse my mother with. It was easy to manage if it was a school day, because then I had ostensibly been to school and hadn't any bats. She was not a suspicious person, but full of trust and confidence; and when I said 'There's something in my coat-pocket for you', she would put her hand in. But she always took it out again, herself; I didn't have to tell her. It was remarkable, the way she couldn't learn to like private bats. The more experience she had, the more she could not change her views.

I think she was never in the cave in her life; but everybody else went there. Many excursion-parties came from considerable distances up and down the river to visit the cave. It was miles in extent, and was a tangled wilderness of narrow and lofty clefts and passages. It was an easy place to get lost in; anybody could do it – including the bats. I got lost in it myself, along with a lady, and our last candle burned down to almost nothing before we glimpsed the search-party's lights winding about in the distance.

The country schoolhouse was three miles from my uncle's farm. It stood in a clearing in the woods, and would hold about twenty-five boys and girls. We attended the school with more or less regularity once or twice a week, in summer, walking to it in the cool of the morning by the forest paths, and back in the gloaming at the end of the day. All the pupils brought their dinners in baskets – corn dodger, buttermilk and other good things – and sat in the shade of the trees at noon and ate them. It is the part of my education which I look back upon with the most satisfaction. My first visit to the school was when I was seven. A strapping girl of fifteen, in the customary sunbonnet and calico dress, asked me if I 'used tobacco' – meaning did I chew it. I said, no. It roused her scorn. She reported me to all the crowd and said –

'Here is a boy seven years old who can't chew tobacco.'

By the looks and comments which this produced, I realized that I was a degraded object; I was cruelly ashamed of myself. I determined to reform. But I only made myself sick; I was not able to learn to chew tobacco. I learned to smoke fairly well, but that did not conciliate anybody, and I remained a poor thing, and characterless. I longed to be respected, but I never was able to rise. Children have but little charity for each other's defects.

As I have said, I spent some part of every year at the farm until I was twelve or thirteen years old. The life which I led there with my cousins was full of charm, and so is the memory of it yet. I can call back the solemn twilight and mystery of the deep woods, the earthy smells, the faint odors of the wild flowers, the sheen of rain-washed foliage, the rattling clatter of drops when the wind shook the trees, the far-off hammering of wood-peckers and the muffled drumming of wood-pheasants in the remoteness of the forest, the snap-shot glimpses of disturbed wild creatures skurrying through the grass, – I can call it all back and make it as real as it ever was, and as blessed. I can call back the prairie, and its loneliness and peace, and a vast hawk hanging motionless in the sky, with his wings spread wide and the blue of the vault showing through the fringe of their end-feathers. I can see the woods in their autumn dress, the oaks purple, the hickories washed with gold, the maples and the sumachs luminous with crimson fires, and I can hear the rustle made by the fallen leaves as we plowed through them. I can see the blue clusters of wild grapes hanging amongst the foliage of the saplings, and I remember the taste of them and the smell. I know how the wild blackberries looked, and how they tasted; and the same with the pawpaws, the hazelnuts and the persimmons; and I can feel the thumping rain, upon my head, of hickory nuts and walnuts when we were out in the frosty dawns to scramble for them with the pigs, and the gusts of wind loosed them and sent them down. I know the stain of blackberries, and how pretty it is; and I know the stain of walnut hulls, and how little it minds soap and water; also what grudged experience it had of either of them. I know the taste of maple sap, and when to gather it, and how to arrange the troughs and the delivery-tubes, and how to boil down the juice, and how to hook the sugar after it is made; also how much better hooked sugar tastes than any that is honestly come by, let bigots say what they will. I know how a prize watermelon looks when it is sunning its fat rotundity among pumpkin vines and 'simblins'; I know how to tell when it is ripe without 'plugging' it; I know how inviting it looks when it is cooling itself in a tub of water

under the bed, waiting; I know how it looks when it lies on the table
in the sheltered great floor-space between house and kitchen, and
the children gathered for the sacrifice and their mouths watering;
I know the crackling sound it makes when the carving knife enters
its end, and I can see the split fly along in front of the blade as the
knife cleaves its way to the other end; I can see its halves fall apart and
display the rich red meat and the black seeds, and the heart standing
up, a luxury fit for the elect; I know how a boy looks, behind a yard-
long slice of that melon, and I know how he feels; for I have been
there. I know the taste of the watermelon which has been honestly
come by, and I know the taste of the watermelon which has been
acquired by art. Both taste good, but the experienced know which
tastes best. I know the look of green apples and peaches and pears
on the trees, and I know how entertaining they are when they are
inside of a person. I know how ripe ones look when they are piled
in pyramids under the trees, and how pretty they are and how vivid
their colors. I know how a frozen apple looks, in a barrel down cellar
in the winter time, and how hard it is to bite, and how the frost makes
the teeth ache, and yet how good it is, notwithstanding. I know the
disposition of elderly people to select the specked apples for the
children, and I once knew ways to beat the game. I know the look
of an apple that is roasting and sizzling on a hearth on a winter's
evening, and I know the comfort that comes of eating it hot, along
with some sugar and a drench of cream. I know the delicate art and
mystery of so cracking hickory nuts and walnuts on a flatiron with a
hammer that the kernels will be delivered whole, and I know how the
nuts, taken in conjunction with winter apples, cider and doughnuts,
make old people's old tales and old jokes sound fresh and crisp and
enchanting, and juggle an evening away before you know what went
with the time. I know the look of Uncle Dan'l's kitchen as it was on
privileged nights when I was a child, and I can see the white and black
children grouped on the hearth, with the firelight playing on their
faces and the shadows flickering upon the walls, clear back toward
the cavernous gloom of the rear, and I can hear Uncle Dan'l telling

the immortal tales which Uncle Remus Harris was to gather into his book and charm the world with, by and by; and I can feel again the creepy joy which quivered through me when the time for the ghost story of the 'Golden Arm' was reached – and the sense of regret, too, which came over me, for it was always the last story of the evening, and there was nothing between it and the unwelcome bed.

I can remember the bare wooden stairway in my uncle's house, and the turn to the left above the landing, and the rafters and the slanting roof over my bed, and the squares of moonlight on the floor, and the white cold world of snow outside, seen through the curtainless window. I can remember the howling of the wind and the quaking of the house on stormy nights, and how snug and cosy one felt, under the blankets, listening; and how the powdery snow used to sift in, around the sashes, and lie in little ridges on the floor, and make the place look chilly in the morning, and curb the wild desire to get up – in case there was any. I can remember how very dark that room was, in the dark of the moon, and how packed it was with ghostly stillness when one woke up by accident away in the night, and forgotten sins came flocking out of the secret chambers of the memory and wanted a hearing; and how ill chosen the time seemed for this kind of business; and how dismal was the hoo-hooing of the owl and the wailing of the wolf, sent mourning by on the night wind.

I remember the raging of the rain on that roof, summer nights, and how pleasant it was to lie and listen to it, and enjoy the white splendor of the lightning and the majestic booming and crashing of the thunder. It was a very satisfactory room; and there was a lightning rod which was reachable from the window, an adorable and skittish thing to climb up and down, summer nights, when there were duties on hand of a sort to make privacy desirable.

I remember the 'coon and 'possum-hunts, nights, with the negroes, and the long marches through the black gloom of the woods, and the excitement which fired everybody when the distant bay of an experienced dog announced that the game was treed; then the wild scramblings and stumblings through briars and bushes and over roots to get to the spot; then the lighting of a fire and the felling of the tree, the joyful frenzy of the dogs and the negroes, and the weird picture it all made in the red glare – I remember it all well, and the delight that every one got out of it, except the 'coon.

I remember the pigeon seasons, when the birds would come in millions, and cover the trees and by their weight break down the branches. They were clubbed to death with sticks; guns were not necessary, and were not used. I remember the squirrel-hunts, and prairie-chicken hunts, and wild turkey hunts, and all that; and how we turned out, mornings, while it was still dark, to go on these expeditions, and how chilly and dismal it was, and how often I regretted that I was well enough to go. A toot on a tin horn brought twice as many dogs as were needed, and in their happiness they raced and scampered about, and knocked small people down, and made no end of unnecessary noise. At the word, they vanished away toward the woods, and we drifted silently after them in the melancholy gloom. But presently the gray dawn stole over the world, the birds piped up, then the sun rose and poured light and comfort all around, everything was fresh and dewy and fragrant, and life was a boon again. After three hours of tramping we arrived back wholesomely tired, overladen with game, very hungry, and just in time for breakfast. ■

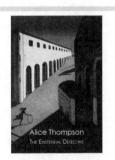

CONTRIBUTORS

Leila Aboulela is the author of a collection of short stories, *Coloured Lights*, and two novels, *The Translator* and, most recently, *Minaret* (Bloomsbury/Grove Atlantic). Her new novel, *Lyrics Alley* (Weidenfeld & Nicolson/Grove Atlantic), will be published in January 2011.

Chimamanda Ngozi Adichie is the author of two novels, *Purple Hibiscus* (2003) and *Half of a Yellow Sun*, which won the 2007 Orange Prize for Fiction. *The Thing Around Your Neck*, a collection of short stories, was published in 2009 (Fourth Estate/Knopf).

Nicholas Christopher has published five novels, including *Veronica* and *A Trip to the Stars* (Bantam/Dial Press), and eight volumes of poetry. A new novel, *Tiger Rag* (Dial Press) and a children's novel, *The True Adventures of Nicolò Zen* (Knopf) are forthcoming.

Hal Crowther won the H. L. Mencken Award for Writing in

1992. He is the author of the essay collection *Gather at the River* (LSU), 2006 finalist for the National Books Critics Circle prize in criticism. His next collection is entitled *Departures*.

Janine di Giovanni is the author of five books, most recently *The Place at the End of the World* (Bloomsbury). Her memoir of life as a war reporter, *Ghosts by Daylight*, will be published next year (Bloomsbury/Knopf).

Colin Grant is a BBC radio producer and an independent historian. His first book, *Negro with a Hat: The Rise and Fall of Marcus Garvey*, was published in 2008 (Jonathan Cape/Oxford University Press). *I&I: The Natural Mystics*, a group biography of the original Wailers, will be published in 2011 (Jonathan Cape/Norton). *Bageye at the Wheel*, a memoir, from which 'Lino' is taken, will be published in 2012.

Seamus Heaney was born in Northern Ireland. He has published poetry, criticism and translations that have established him as one of the leading poets of his generation. In 1995 he was awarded the Nobel Prize in Literature. The poem in this issue will appear in *Human Chain*, published in September (Faber & Faber/Farrar, Straus and Giroux).

Elizabeth McCracken was selected as one of *Granta*'s Best Young American Novelists in 1996. The author of two novels and a short-story collection, her most recent work is a memoir entitled *An Exact Replica of a Figment of My Imagination* (Jonathan Cape/Little, Brown).

Iris Murdoch (1919–99), a Dublin-born British author and philosopher, won the Booker Prize in 1978 for *The Sea, the Sea*. She is the author of twenty-six novels. Many hundreds of her letters and books from her Oxford and London libraries have been acquired by the Centre for Iris Murdoch Studies at Kingston University and are held in the Murdoch Archives there.

Joseph O'Neill lives in New York City and is the author of three novels, including *Netherland* (Harper Perennial/Vintage), which was awarded the 2009 PEN/Faulkner Award for Fiction, and of a family history, *Blood-Dark Track* (Granta/Vintage).

Peter Orner is the author of *The Second Coming of Mavala Shikongo* (Little, Brown), finalist for the *Los Angeles Times* Book Prize, and *Esther Stories* (Mariner). His new novel, *Love and Shame and Love* (Little, Brown), will be out next year.

Adrienne Rich is an American poet, essayist, critic and feminist. She has published numerous collections and is the recipient of many awards including the Lannan Lifetime Achievement Award, the National Book Award, a MacArthur Fellowship, and the 2010 Griffin Poetry Prize Lifetime Recognition Award. Her collection *Tonight No Poetry Will Serve: Poems 2007-2010* is forthcoming in January 2011 (W. W. Norton).

Richard Russo is the author of seven novels, including the Pulitzer Prize-winning *Empire Falls*, and one short-story collection. His most recent work, *That Old Cape Magic*, was published in 2009 (Chatto & Windus/Knopf).

Ian Teh's photographs were highly commended for the Prix Pictet in 2009. His book, *Undercurrents* (Timezone 8), was published in celebration of his solo show in Beijing. Work from his current project, *Traces*, will be featured at the Royal Academy Summer Exhibition.

Mark Twain, born Samuel Langhorne Clemens in 1835, requested that his autobiography remain unpublished until one hundred years after his death in 1910. 'The Farm' comes from the *Autobiography of Mark Twain, Volume I*, which will be published by the University of California Press in November 2010.

Claire Vaye Watkins is a Nevadan and a Presidential Fellow at the Ohio State University.

Her work has appeared in *Hobart, The Hopkins Review, Las Vegas Weekly* and *Ploughshares.*

Contributing Editors
Diana Athill, Peter Carey, Sophie Harrison, Isabel Hilton, Blake Morrison, John Ryle, Lucretia Stewart, Edmund White